by S. J. Perelman

DAWN GINSBERGH'S REVENGE
STRICTLY FROM HUNGER
LOOK WHO'S TALKING
THE DREAM DEPARTMENT
CRAZY LIKE A FOX
KEEP IT CRISP
ACRES AND PAINS
WESTWARD HA!
LISTEN TO THE MOCKING BIRD
THE SWISS FAMILY PERELMAN
THE ILL-TEMPERED CLAVICHORD
PERELMAN'S HOME COMPANION
THE ROAD TO MILTOWN
THE MOST OF S. J. PERELMAN
THE RISING GORGE
THE BEAUTY PART
CHICKEN INSPECTOR NO. 23
BABY, IT'S COLD INSIDE
VINEGAR PUSS
EASTWARD HA!

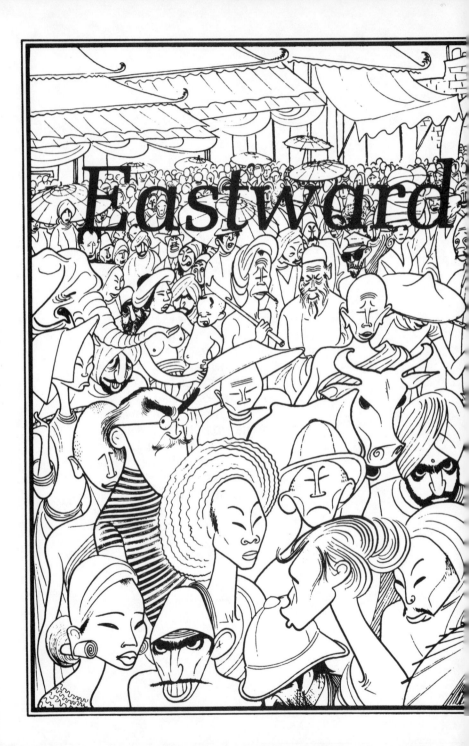

Ha!

S. J. Perelman

Simon and Schuster / New York

Published by Simon and Schuster
A Division of Gulf & Western Corporation
Simon & Schuster Building
Rockefeller Center
1230 Avenue of the Americas
New York, New York 10020
Designed by Edith Fowler
Manufactured in the United States of America
1 2 3 4 5 6 7 8 9 10

Library of Congress Cataloging in Publication Data

Perelman, Sidney Joseph, date.
    Eastward ha!

    1. Travel—Anecdotes, facetiae, satire, etc.   I.   Title.
PS3531.E6544E3   818'.5'207   77-8388

ISBN 0-671-22855-2

Acknowledgment is due to Travel & Leisure, in whose pages
the major part of the text has appeared.

For Chaim Raphael

Contents

1   Looking for Pussy   11

2   Paris on Five Dolors a Day   29

3   The Millennium, and What They Can Do
      with It   43

4   The Nearer the East, the Shorter the Shrift   56

5   Unshorn Locks and Bogus Bagels   68

6   The Vintner Buys the Rolls Nobody Eats   80

7   Rosy and Sleazy, or Dream and Reality
      in Asia   92

8   To One Cup of Java, Add One Snootful
      of Tahiti   103

9   Back Home in Tinseltown   115

1

Looking for Pussy

Thirty-three thousand feet over Cape Ann, high above cumulus that streamed away under the fuselage like dissolving yoghurt, I knew for a certainty that someone was tickling my nose with a feather. For an instant or two I lay rigid, trying to puzzle it out. Could it be the taller of the stewardesses, the blue-eyed brunette sporting a pair of the shapeliest legs since Cyd Charisse's? Or was it her colleague, the taffy-haired blonde whose bosom the French salute in the noblest of accolades, *Il y a du monde au balcon*? In that delectable state of eroticism between sleep and waking, it seemed worthwhile to ponder the question, but the tickling persisted and I opened my eyes. A common housefly was dive-bombing me, doubtless attracted by grains of sugar from the Danish I had eaten before boarding at Kennedy. Just as I moved to annihilate it, the incongruity of its presence on a 707 winging east at ten miles a minute arrested the blow. All the resources of en-

11

gineering and computerization had failed to prevent genus *Musca domestica* from accompanying me on my global circuit. And simultaneously, I was reminded of a significant historical parallel. Somewhere in the Southern ocean, as the immortal Captain Joshua Slocum recounted in his journal *Around the World in the Sloop Spray,* he was touched to discover that his loneliness was ephemeral. An intrepid spider in the cabin was spinning sidewise while he spun forward, and the knowledge of their companionship inspirited him for the rigors that lay ahead.

"Can I get you anything—Scotch, gin, brandy?" My brunette handmaid was beckoning seductively from her trolley, and almost drove me off mine as I realized the mirror image. It was that sorceress of the silent screen, Priscilla Dean, the rangy siren whose dimples had spellbound me in high school as I hung batlike from the arabesques of a Rhode Island nickelodeon. Heralded by a mighty organ sting, it came to me that this whole trip was going to be dipped in magic, a tape run backward embodying all my earliest fantasies.

"Brandy?" I stammered, bashful under her luminous orbs. "But it's so early in the morning—I just had breakfast."

"We're on London time." A dazzling smile that outshone Priscilla's. "It's four o'clock."

"In that case I'll have a double," I said decisively. Once bolstered with cognac, I figured, I could nerve myself to propose marriage within half an hour.

"Sound thinking, sir," she approved. She was a good scout, I could tell; we were suited to each other. The prospect grew even rosier as the level in my glass dropped. What if I *was* a bit long in the tooth? I could take up lotto to compensate for our difference in age, and she crewel work. After all, it was common knowledge that Daddy Browning and Peaches had enjoyed good vibes until those tabloid bastards besmirched their romance.

By the time the second highball was finished, I dismissed as premature the idea of asking the captain to marry us during the flight, and settled down with the cool detachment brandy always produces to review the schedule I'd set for the coming months. It was fraught with promise: the United Kingdom, France, Russia, Israel, Iran, Kashmir, Hunza, Java, Borneo, Tahiti, and finally, the most primitive civilization of all, the Holly-wood colony I had known in the thirties. There were also exciting variations along the route. Like a fellow scenario-writer in my past, I might tarry awhile in a Tibetan lamasery and have daily issues of the *Hollywood Reporter* brought over the Himalayas by muleback. I might hunt up Djem-Djem, the dainty Siamese beauty wooed in Bangkok in 1947, whose porcelain figure I was sure hadn't altered a jot or tittle since we parted. There was, preeminently, the Indonesian project left unfinished on my drawing board from 1973: to construct a 70-foot schooner at Dobo in the Aru Islands on which, aided by a crew of swarthy Lascars or Kanakas, I would go blackbirding in the South Moluccas. I wasn't too clear what blackbirding involved, but from bar mitzvah on, I had longed to qualify as a Jewish Robert Louis Stevenson.

The thought of that restless spirit brought me back to the immediate. Scotland, the first segment of my trip, held forth special appeal. The Highland fling I envisioned would be composed of toasted scones, salmon fishing, a stag drive, and the likelihood that I might be handcuffed to a latter-day Madeleine Carroll, combing the moors for a master spy minus his fingertip. Daydreaming over the possibility, I recalled how my colleague James Thurber had derived considerable revenue from his expertise on the subject.

"I can assert without fear of successful contradiction," he used to assert to friends, "that I have seen *The Thirty-Nine Steps* more often than anyone alive, including the director. Thirty-nine times, in fact." Armed with this strange power, he used to haunt a celebrated Manhattan oasis, Jack Bleeck's Artist (sic) and Writers Club, lying in wait for pigeons. When some unsuspecting civilian chanced by his table where (for example) twilight sleep was under discussion, Thurber would gracefully steer the conversation around to asking whether anybody there had seen Hitchcock's film.

"Oh, boy, *have* I ever!" the patsy would boast. "I must have seen it half a dozen times."

"Fantastic," Thurber commented silkily. "Then you know it by heart. I'm sure you recollect the scene where Robert Donat, on the run, seeks shelter in a crofter's hut."

"Of course," came the answer with a patronizing smile. "The crofter's young wife—played by Peggy Ashcroft, in case you forgot—takes a shine to the fugitive. She persuades her husband to let him stay the night."

"Sir, you have an amazingly retentive memory," Thurber marveled. "She also suggests he be given some food. Do you by any chance remember what the crofter then says to Donat—his exact line of dialogue? I'll bet a sawbuck you don't."

"Wait! Wait!" the other would chant, feverishly ransacking his brain. "M-m-m . . . m-m-m—yes, I do!" Out came the wallet. "For ten dollars, you said? O.K., Thurber, put up your dough!" The bet posted, the sacrificial lamb would inhale and respond, "The crofter says to him, '*Do you eat herring?*'"

Thurber's triumphant cackle echoed from the rafters. "You lose, brother! The actual line read, '*Do you eat THE herring?*' That's the Scottish idiom!"

I must have sunk into reverie, resurrecting those brave days of Prohibition when Jack Kirkland of *Tobacco Road* fame assaulted Richard Watts, the drama critic, with his tiny fists, and the aforementioned Thurber, ever a gallant with the ladies, flung a drink into Lillian Hellman's face in Tony's, when a conversation in the seat behind mine galvanized me. Someone with a youthful tenor voice was ventilating an abstruse medical problem to his older seatmate.

"Do you administer it by mouth or by hypodermic?"

"No, it's quicker with the needle. I give them a shot in the butt and plant them outside. If there's no stupor or tachycardia in ten minutes, my nurse sends them home."

"Gee, that's risky. A fireman I injected—a big strapping guinea from the Bronx—went into shock before I could paste on a Band-Aid. I had to use ten c.c.'s of adrenaline."

"You should have let him lie on the floor and seen your next patient."

"That's fine if you have two consultation rooms. It undermines people, a guy stretched out like a cadaver while you're diagnosing them."

"You'll get over that. I was the same when I first set up practice. Say, these are great—do you want another?"

"Right. Listen, Max, how many chairs in your waiting room? I've got fourteen."

"Too many—makes your office look like a meat market. Four, five is plenty. And watch the *National Geographics* you strew around, they shouldn't be too recent. Better if the patient's half-comatose when you examine."

"Especially the dames," his junior added slyly.

"Quiet, for chrissake," the elder warned. "That's my wife across the aisle."

My blood congealed; the stars in their courses, visibly, had programmed me into the midst of a charter group. Between the movies and the meal,

Gott sei danke, the doctors themselves became anesthetized. In the all-too-brief interval before touching down at Heathrow, my blue-eyed goddess, regrettably, was too busy to plight our troth. Nevertheless, as she bade me farewell at the exit hatch, trig in her uniform and erect as a young fir tree, her face bore a look of quite extraordinary devotion. I felt I could lean on her should I ever need support. But that, of course, was academic since I never got her number. Perhaps it was because the moment she'd seen me, she instinctively got mine.

It was on the third day after my arrival in Edinburgh that I remembered Fiona's injunction about the party I was to ring up. Fiona herself was Scots, sprung from a prominent northern clan, and altogether smashing, but her job in London excluded any possibility of joining me on a motor excursion around Scotland. "The person you absolutely must meet, though," she said when I asked for guidance, "is Sir Alasdair Pech-and-Schwebyll of that Ilk. Yes, that's actually his name. Tremendous expert on genealogy and a real cutie. I'll phone him tonight—he'll put you in the picture as nobody else can."

My fleeting survey of Edinburgh charmed me— in contrast to Glasgow, the only city I knew north of the Tweed, its gracious squares and eighteenth-century facades readily explained all the superlatives I'd heard. After an obligatory ascent to the Castle that left me limp with fatigue, I was drawn by some instinct for self-preservation to the Café Royal, whose tiled murals of early navigation and notables like Faraday, Stephenson, Watt, Caxton, and Daguerre, viewed over a dram of Glenfiddich, restored the ichor in my veins. An ensuing trip to the Museum of Childhood in the Royal Mile proved an even more enchanting experience. It revived tonic memories of adolescence that (I freely confess it) bathed my face in tears.

While sponging them away, I remembered other aspects of Edinburgh I had vowed to investigate. There was the legend of the body-snatchers, preserved in the well-known verse,

> Up the close and down the stair
> But and ben with Burke and Hare,
> Burke's the butcher, Hare's the thief,
> And Knox the boy that buys the beef.

It was distressing to learn from a constable that the mews frequented by the infamous pair existed no longer. As for Dr. Joseph Bell, the preceptor on whom Conan Doyle had patterned Sherlock Holmes, the distinguished anatomist would now be one hundred and thirty-five and too enfeebled to question about the science of deduction. It was just as well, perhaps; a similar genuflection of mine to the great detective had resulted in embarrassment. Once, while resident in London, I ventured into Alexander Smith & Sons in New Oxford Street and asked to be shown a Penang lawyer, the kind of walking stick owned by the monstrous Dr. Grimesby Roylott in

The *Adventure of the Speckled Band.* The clerk dredged up a martyred sigh. "Forgive me, sir, but you're the ninth American who's made that request this year," he said. "It burdens my day no end. I've begged Mr. Smith to post a notice in the window."

Sir Alasdair's voice, when I finally reached him on the blower, sounded resigned. "Ah, yes, that blackguard who writes books," he said. "Fiona warned me. Well, I'm five miles outside Milchadic at a place called Auchundvay, and when you drive in, an Irish wolfhound may seize you by the throat. But it's sheer bluff, she's only a baby."

I got into his early Georgian chalet with no impairment but a wet sleeve, and found Sir Alasdair sipping a pre-luncheon drink with a friend. He was a sparkling-eyed gentleman in his sixties, unexpectedly clad in a nightshirt and tasseled cap and somewhat reminiscent of Max Beerbohm at Rapallo.

"Been up since dawn completing an article on Rokeach, my ancestor, the Thane of Nyafat," he said. "This is my house guest, the Honorable Auberon Rachmonnies. He'll do the honors whilst I go up and change."

Rachmonnies, a handsome dog of about forty in kilt, sporran, and the traditional skean dhu, or dagger, in his hose, arose creakily to extend a tremulous hand. "I'm not very well," he apologized. "Picked up a chill on the liver, doubtless. You'll take whiskey, of course?" I observed him channel it with some difficulty into a tumbler and noticed that he repressed a shudder. His next remark furnished a clue to the ailment. "I'm sticking to Guinness for the present," he said dolefully. "You're over here on the North Sea oil project, I expect. What part of Texas are you from?"

I thought my geographical origins too intricate to explain, and asked where he himself dwelt. He was currently based in a village northeast of Edinburgh whose pub he was certain I would relish. Moreover, he added, if I were free on the morrow, he would give me lunch at his club in Queen Street, near my hotel. This was the Scots hospitality Fiona had foreshadowed, and I warmed to it. Under repeated draughts of malt at lunch, I warmed even further. Pech-and-Schwebyll of that Ilk, now resplendent in figured neckerchief and nile-green hacking jacket, discoursed spiritedly on his two favorite topics, genealogy and usquebaugh.

"Perelman? Perelman?" he repeated, wrinkling his nose. "Balderdash—no such name in the College of Heralds. Yes, there were a few ending in 'man,' but nobody uses them nowadays. More than likely he's some kind of spiv," he cautioned Rachmonnies. "Still, you might take him in hand. Show him Marchmont, Kinross, Balblair House, Inverary Castle, a few of the clan strongholds in the west. Drink up, boy!" he commanded me. "This Glenfusel is the best whiskey in Perthshire. The water comes from a burn the

Camerons tapped in 1351 to rinse their wet wash."

Toward dusk, I felt my way out, regained my bed, and awoke at eleven the next morning to word that Rachmonnies had arrived to honor his promise. Over brunch, seeing that he clung somberly to Guinness, I inquired about the state of his liver.

"Only middling," he sighed. "But I'm worried about something else. I'm told my cat's been looking for me."

I was sure the man had lost his marbles. "What did you say?"

"My cat, Magellan—named after the explorer. I left him with a couple a year ago when I went off to Italy, and they claim he's looking for me."

"Where is this couple?"

"In Lackadaisy, the village where I'm based. They don't have him, though. He's run off—hiding in a farmer's granary."

"I still don't twig. Is he asking people the whereabouts of his master, the Marquis of Carabas?"

He shrugged. "Who knows? Cats have a way of communicating these things. All I know is, I've got to find him, and as I'm rather frail at the moment, I could use your help."

"In what way?"

"Well, I thought if you'd scrounge around for a proper basket and fetch it down, I'd show you the pub I mentioned and then we'll snare Pussy."

All of which may explain why, later that day, 21

an American tourist with pebble glasses and a ginger moustache happened into a luggage shop on Princes Street seeking what he imprecisely termed a cat-house. As for the successive stages by which he reached Lackadaisy in a hired car, driving perilously on the wrong side of the road, that can be left to the imagination of underwriters. The vaunted pub, the Star & Kreplach, turned out to be as commonplace as any in my experience—nobody has ever clarified the Briton's adoration of saloons and his Talmudic exegesis of their virtues—and our search for Magellan equally fruitless. When last seen, the animal had been trotting after a kid named Dick Whittington, said to be headed for London. Out of our quest, however, there evolved a proposal from Rachmonnies to chauffeur us on a round of celebrated houses owned by the gentry, in all of which we would be greeted with acclamation and feasting. The strain on my credit card, as I foresaw it, would be minimal, the pilgrimage enriching. I leaped at the opportunity, and armed with maps, a flashlight, and a restorative (Bendrick's Military & Sporting Chocolate, Ideal Sustenance in an Emergency), we hit the road.

As we progressed southward into Berwickshire toward Ichvaisnit Grange, the fief of Gornicht Kinhelfinn, the Scourge of the Bog, I began forming a mosaic out of the bits of information my companion let drop about himself. A product of Harrow and Cambridge, he was descended from some liege of James II who held either the king's robes or his lobes—I could not tell which, as the car hit a stone at that juncture. Apart from a year of naval service on a minesweeper in the Western Approaches, clearing away empties of Chivas Regal, Rachmonnies had never done a day's work in his life and gloried in it. He was unmarried, but over the years had courted innumerable daughters of the peerage. He thought the reason he had escaped wedlock was that none of them shared his interest in science.

"Oh? What branch are you involved in?"

"The spirits, chiefly. I've done quite a bit of research on the subject."

"Parapsychology?" I queried, electrified. "So have I. A friend of mine, Julie Newmar, and I were once horsing around with her Ouija board—"

"I mean the distilled kind," he put in impatiently. "Their effect on body chemistry. Have you heard the latest theory? They've found that as long as one continues drinking, he's safe. It's the sudden stop that's fatal—the strain on the heart, you know. Many a chap who's pushing up the daisies would be here now if he hadn't quit. As a result," he concluded, "I've learned to protect myself. That's why I'm on Guinness at this time."

"Yes, that jibes with my premedical training."

"Oh, you've worked in hospitals?" Suddenly he was more animated than I had yet seen him. "Then you'll be interested in my discovery last year in a Swiss clinic. The doctors there have worked out a radical new technique—they drink along with the patient to ascertain what causes the craving. In my case, they decided it was vestigial, a desire for the warm security of the prenatal state, and strongly advised me to carry on. Said it might damage the nerve ends if I knocked off."

Apparently he'd heeded their counsel, for in the same breath, a van piled with hay shot out of a road beside us and Rachmonnies, in a reflex worthy of Tazio Nuvolari, slewed around it. I was still fuschia-colored, palpitant with Cheyne-Stokes breathing, when we rumbled across the cattle grids of the lane into Ichvaisnit Grange. There was a disconcerting pause on the oval while my guide conferred at length with a sour-faced menial at the door.

"Hard cheese," he said, resuming his seat. "Says he has orders not to admit anyone. Gornicht's in Majorca, and Clarissa, my cousin, is down south with a poisoned foot."

"I saw two faces peeping at us behind a curtain upstairs."

"Ah, very likely—I broke a Venetian glass candelabra of theirs last time I stayed. Well, no matter, I'm sure there'll be a bed for us at Voss Tutmendaw, Sir Roderick de Momzer's place. It has two hundred rooms."

Undoubtedly it had, but affixed to the gate-house was a large sign in Gaelic. *"A finsterra yorr in baina, shikker,"* it read. *"Mir chollischt avec mit dein narischkeit. Zolst lig'n in draird"*— which Rachmonnies translated as "Sorry. Full up." We bivouacked that night at the confluence of three arteries where giant lorries whipped past each other like flyers in Con Colleano's aerial troupe. Dining on snacks in the hotel bar amid rustics braying over a rugger match, I noticed that the regimen of Guinness had undergone revision; the invalid had graduated to three fingers of Glencordite, an amber witch that smoked on release from the dispenser. Calvinist disapproval, I reflected as I sank into bed, was juvenile under the circumstances. My destiny was non-negotiable, yoked as it was to a stranger's ganglia and the vagaries of his endocrine system. The die was cast; above the thundering lorries, I could hear the croupier's decree, *"Les jeux sont faits."*

Our trajectory now swerved northwest into the Highlands, an area the man claimed to know like the back of his hand—which member, by the way, gave increasing evidence of *paralysis agitans*. Once in the glens, the roads grew steep and demanded caution, but the higher we climbed, the more obsessive grew Rachmonnies' preoccupation with stimulants. Even the ruins of a castle perched on a crag stirred memories.

"Belonged to Ivor Horseradish, the Red Chrane," he noted. "It's a two-hundred-foot drop from the portcullis into the gorge. That reminds me—I once fell out of a third-story window at Jesus College. Lucky I'd had a few or I wouldn't have survived. . . . Have I told you about protocol wafers?"

My attention was distracted by a ravine we had almost plunged into. "No, what are they?"

"An invention of mine—a biscuit that gives foreigners the know-how to behave in our midst. Which direction to pass the port, what plaids not to wear, the really important titles—that sort of thing. You dissolve one of these wafers, preferably in a little whiskey, and straightaway you're clued in."

"There's a bloody fortune in it. I'll take the American dealership."

"I say, that's very sporting of you. By the way, could you loan me thirty-seven quid for a day or so? I'm a bit short."

It puzzled me why he needed paper currency at that altitude, unless to construct a box kite. "Wee-ll, all right," I said, unzipping my money belt, "but that makes forty-one pounds—with Pussy's basket."

"You'll get it back in Edinburgh, honor bright."

The word of a clansman whose forebears had fought at Flodden was good enough for me. On the outskirts of the next village, he popped into a quaint old inn whose charred roof was being re-thatched. After a quarter of an hour he emerged, wiping his lips. "That'll quash the case for now," he declared jovially. "O.K., off to Manor Sheviss, the seat of the Homintashes. They usually mount a pheasant shoot when I drop by."

His intuition was incorrect; its battlements were ringed around by half a hundred gillies with shotguns at the ready and steely-eyed determination to carry out their orders. In the following three days, we saw countless deer parks and moats, but never the castles they graced. Their owners, invariably, were stricken with black-water fever or lost in the Mato Grosso or were thinning at Bad Ischl; how the House of Lords ever achieved a quorum that week was an enigma. Consequently, in the seesaw course we traversed between Lock Tay, Ben Alder, and the Firth of Lorn, we were thrown back on a series of hostels that surpassed nightmare. These were totally devoid of heat, staffed by madmen, and sunk in apathy, and their cuisine offered only barbarities like pig's trotters, drumheads masquerading as beef, and blood puddings. I retired nightly with a hot-water bottle to pen entries in my diary that rivaled Scott's at the Pole; Rachmonnies, with a cold glass, sat in the bar humming "The Bonnets of Bonnie Dundee" and chuckling dementedly.

At Oban, the port in Argyll where one takes the ferry to the Isle of Mull, we did not take the ferry to the Isle of Mull. My friend's behavior at the wheel became too prankish to ignore; having nearly lofted two old ladies over a hedge, he subjected them to a tirade and fell in the street. His liquefaction left me only one alternative—to abandon the car and decant him back to Edinburgh by rail. On board the train, fortified by a snooze and two mugs of Guinness, he managed to scrawl a shaky cheque for the promised £41.00.

"Just pass it through my bank in Charing Cross, old boy," he directed with a princely wave in parting. His eyes sagged like a basset hound's under his tam-o'-shanter. "I reckon we'll see each other one day in London or elsewhere, won't we?"

I hope to. I'd like to show him the tasteful form marked "Refer to drawer" stapled to his cheque and sent back to me. The smell of burning rubber, whether from our journey or his cheque, still lingers in my nose. Ofttimes, puffing on my briar and gazing into the flames, I ask myself why Pussy was looking for him. What did he have on Rachmonnies that I never found out? Only Holmes, or better yet, Dr. Joseph Bell, could have told me, but I got to Scotland too late for that.

2

Paris on
Five Dolors a Day

"Is all in readiness, then, to welcome back that acclaimed boulevardier, *Feinschmecker,* and Yankee globe-trotter which he is without peer in this century if one overlook Wilfred Thesiger, Henri de Monfried, and Freya Stark?"

The speaker was none other than his tall elegance Valéry Giscard d'Estaing, the President of France; and his council of ministers, assembled around the conference table in the Elysée Palace, was instantly on the qui vive. Every man jack of them knew that as sure as God made little green apple pies (*tartes aux pommes*), Giscard had pledged himself to assure a memorable reception for the American, to sustain the nation's highest traditions of hospitality and *la gloire.* Should anyone there fail in the slightest to discharge his share of responsibility, his head would roll in the sand and never again taste another *Coquille St. Jacques, Boeuf en Daube,* or *Ile Flottante de Ma Tante Rose.* It was enough to stiffen the resolve of the most apathetic bureaucrat, and there were plenty of them there.

"Everything is complete, *mon Président*," spoke up the Minister of the Interior, Kidneys, and Chitterlings. "The Deuxième Bureau reports that even now Perelman is en route from Orly to the Left Bank, where, as is his lifelong custom, he has reserved a room in a second-rate hotel. Nothing can go wrong; barring the unforeseen, our game plan functions like a well-oiled machine."

"Then the rest is in the lap of the gods," quoth Giscard with a typically Gallic shrug. "So let us adjourn to our midday feed. Quaffing the good red wine of France, we can be certain that this longtime visitor to our shores will find our fiendishness unchanged, all the torments a Torquemada could invent still bugging him."

His words lagged behind the actuality. At that precise moment, I was already registered at the Hotel of the Cheap Valises in Montparnasse, readying a bundle of wash to carry out under my jacket. Friends in England had warned me that hotel laundry bills here were exorbitant, and I was too travel-wise to waste money on superfluities. I latched the bundle to a hook in the bathroom, divested myself of my threads, and prepared to shower. Forthwith I discovered (as one should have remembered) that soap was never supplied in France, fats being conserved exclusively for soups. A cake of violet Camay filched in London, however, solved the impasse, and *30* whistling the clarinet passage from Benny Goodman's "Stealin' Apples," I ascended the platform the small bathtub was mounted on.

Like clockwork, the first phase of the government's stratagem went into action. The three rickety steps, cunningly designed of unequal height, threw me off balance and I lurched forward, striking my nose with volcanic force against the shower taps. For an instant everything went black—not by chance, for simultaneously the power was shut off. A slight pause ensued to give me the illusion of security and proceed with my ablutions; then, as I turned on the cold water to rinse, the ministers applied the hotfoot. A gush of steam jetted from the shower head and I sprang outward in a leap that would shame a Watusi tribesman. Here the disparate steps and my soapy feet combined for maximum effect. I described a half gainer, slithered across the tiled floor, and landed upside down against the bidet.

"*Mot de Cambronne*," I murmured thickly. "Can my zodiac be all at sixes and sevens? Venus was supposed to enter my house, not Vulcan. Well, anyway, better get shaved."

Had I been more objective, the coup de grace awaiting me would surely have excited my admiration. The pinchbeck medicine cabinet, stamped out of tin and encased in plastic, had three mirrored doors, which, upon opening, loosed the carpet tacks pinning it to the wall. With a noise like a fragmentation bomb, the whole caboodle fell into the sink, spraying me with spicules of glass. It was three-quarters of an hour before I finished tweezing them out, by which time I had shed more tears than Lillian Gish in her entire screen career.

My reunion with France's mechanical fantasies, however, was incomplete as yet; there was one more affliction in store. Wrapping the soggy bundle of wash in a newspaper, I made for the elevator. Within its frosted glass door, massive enough for a bank vault, lay a flimsy cage with a folding metal gate whose handle was slyly hidden in a recess. As I groped around for it in the interstices, the gate collapsed and bit my fingers with the savagery of a Doberman pinscher. In the same breath, I was jerked forward, the door slammed, and roaring like a 1917 American La France fire engine, the lift plummeted down fifty feet to spew me into the lobby. The concierge and the manager exchanged gratified smiles. It was not the first time guests had been caught sneaking out laundry, but for one to have encased it herringwise in wet newsprint gave the incident a certain panache.

Outdoors all was electric with the bustle of the metropolis on a fine spring afternoon, familiar to any patron of a Shubert operetta. Gendarmes smirked at saucy midinettes out of the pages of La Vie Parisienne, chestnuts from the same source were being hawked by sidewalk vendors, workmen tore up paving in preparation for the tourist influx. I deposited my wash at a blanchisserie that promised to insert plenty of staples in the briefs, and sat down in a bistro to winnow my address book. While I hadn't alerted my friends,

32

there were several in Paris who I knew would be enraptured to see me. All it needed was a phone call.

I speedily found out that it required something else—the magnetism of a Cary Grant and the psychic powers of Sir Oliver Lodge. One of the ladies had married in the interim, the second was in a loony bin, and happy-go-lucky Charlie, while cured of his hobnail liver, reposed under a headstone. A senseless panic overwhelmed me at the prospect of spending the evening alone. But this was *Paris!* People were dancing the cancan, quaffing champagne out of slippers at Maxim's, courting great horizontals like Liane de Pougy, driving britzkas through the Bois de Boulogne. Was I to wind up in a bedroom with striped wallpaper, reading a yellowed Tauchnitz edition of Goethe's *Conversations with Eckermann?* Better the Seine and a suicide's grave—but first let me exhaust every possibility in the address book. . . .

Marvel of marvels, I found her name at last, almost obliterated by a podiatrist's but still legible: Suzy La Généreuse—a dazzler, a pippin, the great tawny cat I had met at Fouquet's two years back. The pouf escorting her, a window dresser at I. Magnin's, said she was a photographer for *Paris-Match*, had worked in Kenya with Howard Hawks, and was mad for scenario writers with little pebble glasses. We had exchanged chaff— not as meaty as the conversations with Eckermann, more exploratory in nature—and agreed to meet later at La Dominique for *ockroshka*. She must have lost the address, though, and what with the baker my phone call aroused in the 16th arrondissement, it was an early evening. Nevertheless, here was her number, and I crossed my fingers as I flew down to the coin box. The woman who answered, a dear old lady, said yes, she was Suzy's grandmother; the little one was living in her *camionnette*—a small truck—in the outskirts and called in hourly for messages. I left word where I was and tottered up to the bar for a grappa. Excitement had me faint.

Three hours later at the hotel, I was about to sack out over a Barbarella comic when a hoarse coloratura voice on the blower brought me to in a flurry of bedclothes. "*Chéri!* Is it really you? Ah, so often have I dreamt of your hands, your lips!" What was the girl talking about? Still, the sentiment was right. "*Attendez*—rush to my *camionnette* at once! I thirst for you."

Nurtured on the pastorals of Watteau and Boucher, I envisioned a daintier setting for our idyll, but only a fool trifles with Dan Cupid, and I was dressed in an instant. The site of our rendezvous, a garage outside Passy, likewise struck me as drab, involving as it did a seventeen-dollar taxi fare. From the grease monkeys lounging there, I learned that Suzy awaited me in a bungalow three blocks distant. She did, if hardly in the state of concupiscence I anticipated. She was curled up on a daybed next to a hairy youth of consuming arrogance whose arm enfolded another and quite unappetizing creature, sultry and unwashed. The blare of country rock was so deafening that it loosened my inlays.

"This is Bébé Lifschitz, the well-known drummer," she called out over the pandemonium. "He's shaking the maracas in Brigitte Bardot's next film." Rising for a negligent peck on my cheek, she added contemptuously, "The other is some *putain* he picked up—I hate her. Well, *mon vieux*," she demanded, hands on hips, "How do I look?"

"A sweetmeat, a morsel for the gods." It sickened me that I could have had such a lapse of taste. "Look, Suzy, I'm desolate but I must get up at seven—I'm flying to Queensland for the sheep trials. The—uh—rams have been accused of some dereliction or other. No, thanks, I don't want any wine."

Her brow blackened. "All right, we'll go." It was obvious I had soured her romance. "I'll drive you back to Paris, but first we have to drop off a bureau at my aunt's."

The *camionnette* housed not only a chiffonier but a gigantic police dog who loudly protested my intrusion. "Don't be afraid—just crouch down on the floor beside Hercule. He's a *mignon*, he protects me from satyrs like yourself."

Rather than deny the soft impeachment, which could have led to bickering, I held my tongue—unlike Hercule, who promptly began slobbering over me. As the kilometers sped by and I fought off his advances, Suzy's mood lightened. She segued into a précis of her activities that impressed me as mingling the effluvia of Rona Barrett with hallucinations uncharted save by Charcot. She had written a screenplay for Belmondo that Truffaut was wild about, as well as a five-minute documentary on Peter Bogdanovich recapping his achievements, and had won second prize in a beauty contest at Gstaad. (The winner, she explained, was a *putain* who had slept with the judges.) We were a block from her aunt's house when Hercule, with a joyful yelp, squirmed out past me, bruising my ankle. It was only after Suzy had manhandled the bureau inside on her powerful shoulders and we were en route again that I grasped the extent of my injury.

"Stop the car!" I cried out, rolling down my sock. "Your animal's crippled me. Look, it's gushing blood—my leg's stiffening—"

She scrutinized the wound by the light of a match. "Absurd," she retorted. "It's a mere scratch. Here, I'll put collodion on it."

"Are you mad? Collodion is nail polish—it seals in the infection! That's the first thing I was taught in premedical school."

"O.K., then, arnica." She smeared on some goodge from a tube and looped a filthy rag over the lesion. "There—you could cross Tanzania on that."

It was that word—Tanzania—that did the damage. Instantly I remembered *The Short Happy Life of Francis Macomber* and saw my fate, dead of gangrene before we ever reached the Porte de Versailles. As we rattled on, a sob welled up in my throat. Was this the way to die, in a *deux-chevaux* piloted by a crazy, the crowning adventure of my life hardly begun? I grabbed Suzy's arm.

"For God's sake, get me to a doctor," I begged. "The throbbing is uncontrollable!" I shuddered. "And what are those shapes fluttering up there? They look like vultures. . . ."

Ultimately, wearied by my pleas, she agreed to stop at an all-night drugstore on the Avenue Wagram. The pimply youth there, a dropout from pharmacy college, further scarified the gash with spirits of ammonia—the upshot being that on gaining my hotel, I limped so badly that I had to be carried up to the room. The well-thumbed copy of Dr. *Proctor's Medical Companion* in my luggage told me I was lucky to be alive.

In the long, slow convalescence that followed, I felt some coddling was due me; suffering had taught me the wisdom of Samuel Smiles's maxim "The branch that bends rarely breaks." I therefore indulged a couple of long-delayed pleasures. At Hilditch & Key's, the fashionable haberdasher in the Rue de Rivoli, I checked out the price of a striped alpaca cardigan I had hungered for since 1968. It now cost $233, and I tartly advised the salesman to hunt up a taxidermist and stuff it. Purged, I went along to an astrologer's in the Rue du Dragon for a preview of the future. Mlle Mouton, who existed only in the imagination of Gian-Carlo Menotti, received me in her sixth-floor walkup. There was enough henna in the hair and kohl rimming her peepers for a summer-stock production of *Zaza*, Leslie Carter's deathless vehicle. The cabinet that the prophetess shared with five thousand lace valentines and a torpid Angora diffused the same bouquet as Mr. Eliot's Grishkin. Her character analysis of my palm was uncanny.

"You can be led but not driven," she divined. "Warmhearted yet miserly, you are as cold as ice. Prouder than a Spanish don, you nonetheless succumb to every pretty ankle, stoop to less than the dust beneath their chariot wheel." She then threw the Tarot pack. "Beauties innumerable have pulled you around by the nose," she recounted accurately. "Let them beware—even a worm can turn. I see two Englishwomen in your life. One, a tall voluptuous blonde, is currently besotted with a Turk. He means her no good, this Ottoman; did she follow him, she would only become a captive in his seraglio. The other, a bewitching crumpet with azure eyes and pageboy hairdo, adores you. She would follow you to the ends of the earth."

My mouth was agape. "What do the stars advise?"

"To fling caution to the winds. Marry them both."

"At once?" I faltered. "That takes mazuma—pelf—"

"*Zut alors!*" One read in her gaze contempt for material concerns. "What does money signify to an American? The hundred francs you are about to disgorge is but *ein Tropfen in der Eimer* [a drop in the bucket]."

"You have a remarkable German accent," I said, impressed.

"*Ja wohl.*" She stroked her bombazine front

complacently. "The last year of the occupation, the Kommandatur gave me a medal for my predictions."

In the final week of my visit, I was confronted with a problem that would have taxed the keenest investigator. Along with the ivory-backed brushes, the crystal stoppers, and the tool to extract chiggers in my toilet kit, I carry two atomizers of an eau de cologne I esteem. What was my dismay one morning to find that they were bonedry after I had filled them the night before. The obvious culprit was the maid, who I knew had been reading my correspondence, since a thread laid across a postcard from some lovesick creature had changed direction. To immure myself in the armoire and trap her was unfeasible, so I hit on an expedient. For a few centimes, I obtained a phial of mosquito repellent from a chemist in the Rue d'Alésia. The old codger feigned ignorance at first of what I sought, necessitating the firm approach used by generations of American tourists.

"Citronella! Citronella!" I shouted, hammering on the showcase. "To chase away skeeters—don't you understand? Any boob knows what that is!"

He did, of course, for the French make their lemonade from it, whether from perversity or avarice. At any rate, I topped up the atomizers and bided my time, sniffing the maid closely whenever she bustled past. Honesty compels me to admit that like all such tactics, the ruse boomeranged. Very shortly, the hotel manager asked me into his office. Without mincing words, he said that the help had become neurasthenic. Unless I quit skulking through the corridors after them, he declared, he would be forced to lay accusations of mopery against me with the Ministry of Justice. To add to my discomfiture, the chemist in the Rue d'Alésia spurned my appeal for a refund on the leftover citronella. Altogether, the affair dramatized how radically France had changed since my student days. The old Bohemian roistering, Hemingway, Sylvia Beach, Proust, the camaraderie—all gone.

My feeling of rue, happily, was dissipated by a quite unforeseen encounter. Shopping around in the Galeries Lafayette for a New York lady who needed a rose-paneled garter belt, some black silk hose, and a whip, I ran into Bootsie Flowers, an American girl on the staff of Vogue I used to date in London. We fell into each other's arms.

"Bootsie, whatever are you doing here out of season?" I queried, mystified. "Everybody but simply everybody is in Biarritz or Sardinia."

"I know—isn't it horrid?" She made a moue. "Work, my dear. I'm researching an article on the bateaux mouches—you know, those sightseeing boats that ply up and down the Seine."

"What fun, darling," I said. "Are you still living with that greenish hophead, Eric what's-his-name?"

"No, with a dwarf, a Touareg from the Atlas Mountains." Suddenly she clutched my arm. "Listen, are you busy later?" I began some excuse about soaking my corns in Cuticura, but she brushed it aside. "I'm in a pickle," she explained. "You see, these *bateaux mouches* folks have gifted me with a scrumptious dinner for two on tonight's cruise, and I'm lacking an escort. Be an angel. It's freebies—wine, music, the works."

Well, weakling that I am, I was touched by her plight, so I gave in, and I must say they laid out the red carpet. An orchid boutonnière for madame, flawless cuisine, five wines, and a table in the prow with a huge centerpiece of freesias that set off Bootsie's fragile beauty. As we sailed upriver past Notre Dame, sipping Dom Perignon to the lilt of javas played by a trio of accordions (the French now have accordions that require no human hands), we both became quite sentimental. I almost forgave her capriciousness in emptying a pail of whitewash over my head when I was wooing her in London, and we became a trifle mushy, but the romance never got off the launch pad, for in the twinkling of an eye, the unimaginable happened.

There was an abrupt, grinding bump that hurled everyone's glassware to the deck, an immediate babble of terrified cries in half a dozen languages mingled with women's shrieks, and our craft yawed about alarmingly. A quick glance sufficed to analyze what had occurred; we had struck the abutment of one of the Seine bridges, doubtless because the pilot, whom I had observed tickling a waitress earlier, was now passed out in the scuppers. A second glance enabled me to assess the gravity of the situation. Our bow was sinking fast—our stern was no chocolate soda either—and in another ten minutes we would all be in Davy Jones's locker.

"*Sauve qui peut,* Bootsie!" I sang out, releasing her hand. "Sorry it had to be this way, but it's every man for himself." As I raced aft, trampling whoever blocked my path, I had the presence of mind to seize a woman's shawl here, a handbag there, so that by the time I reached the melee in the stern, I had the disguise that would save me. "For shame, messieurs!" I shouted at the captain and officers frantically scrambling into the boats. "Have you forgotten the law of the sea? Women and children first!"

Yes, I reflected afterward on the terrace of the Deux Magots while polishing off a final cognac, my Paris sojourn had been one narrow squeak after another, but I had survived, and who knows? Perhaps, like a fine Damascene blade, my nature had been tempered, made nobler in the fires of adversity. Up the Boulevard St. Germain from the Place de l'Odéon there came a bedraggled American girl streaked with mascara, her eyes beady with vengeance, and as she drew closer, I saw it was Bootsie. I flung down a handful of francs and vamoosed into the Rue de l'Université. In the words of wise old Samuel Smiles, who had maxims to excuse any kind of poltroonery, "He who fights and runs away lives to fight another day."

3

The Millennium, and
What They Can Do with It

The clock on the Kremlin tower had just struck eight that sunny May morning when I laid down my razor in Room 423 of the northern block of the Hotel Rossia in Moscow, inhaled deeply, and addressed my reflection in the mirror.

"A thousand apologies, Excellency," I said timidly. "Forgive my speaking to you without an introduction, but I was attracted by your soldierly carriage, a certain—how shall I say?—world-weary charm you exude, an air of having danced too many quadrilles with provincial beauties such as one often sees in a retired colonel of the Preobazhensky Guards conducting a flirtation in the Urals (or possibly the Adrenals or the viscera, where I just felt a sudden *kvetch*). *Tfoo*, how I wander!"

"Perhaps the cat has got your tongue."

"Ha ha! I am, so to speak, not myself today," I confessed, flustered. "What I mean is, you bear a strong resemblance to a man who went to sleep last night in my pajamas but whom I hardly recognize this morning. Can the worst have befallen me, i.e., that I am bonkers?"

"Calm yourself, my dear fellow," came the soothing reply. "All this is just your normal split personality. If memory serves, you arrived here late yesterday to join a fortnight tour of the Soviet Union embracing Moscow, Kiev, Yalta, and Leningrad, did you not?" I nodded. "And in preparation for the trip—to put yourself in the mood for Holy Russia, the land of your forefathers with its vast steppes, birch forests, onion domes, and onion rolls— you reread an entire shelf of Dostoievsky, Tolstoy, Turgenev, and Gogol. Well, you're just down with Slavic logorrhea, a kind of literary gastritis which, as they used to say of another schoolboy complaint, is no worse than a bad cold. Put on your pants and go find your tour."

Reassured, I dusted myself with flea powder, donned my habiliments, and plunged into a labyrinth of corridors, snack bars, post offices, and souvenir shops boiling with East Germans, North Koreans, Bulgarians, and visitors from the fifteen republics of the USSR. Thanks to body English and a pinch of *savate,* I at last reached the vast Pectopah, or restaurant, assigned to my group. Its twenty members were busy engorging a breakfast of cucumbers and little brown torpedoes fried in deep fat called Chicken Kiev, a combination that, taken with warm orange crush, guarantees an immediate peptic ulcer. There were, in fact, a couple of stern-faced women doctors present issuing the ulcer certificate required of all foreign travelers. It was one of two recent advances in Soviet medicine wherewith its scientists boasted they had outstripped China and the West. The other, that they had cured snoring in the bureaucracy, was exploded when Gromyko, at a performance of Yuri Farkriminas' "Sinfonietta for Three Orifices," was heard to emit an unmistakable grunt during the woodwinds. While officially described next day in *Pravda* as a belch, newspaper friends assured me later there was no doubt of its provenance.

"Permit me," I heard a voice directed at me. "I am Natasha, your tour guide. May we have words?" She sat down, and I stole a look. She had ash-blond hair and lovely green eyes. "You came apart on the plane?"

"It sure felt that way," I said. "Maybe I drank too much seltzer in Paris."

"Ah, so you were not with the others from New York." I signified I was a maverick but would abide by the rules. "Very good. Now, one question. As we shall visit many churches, what is your faith?"

"My religion? Money is my God, kiddo. I love it, I adore it, I dream of it."

She pursed her lips. "Yes, yes, you are American—I already know. But you must have a belief, a sect you belong to."

"Well, I do, now you mention it." I pondered. "I am what Puritans scornfully call a womanizer. It's sort of a lay preacher."

"You revere women?" she asked puzzled.

"I worship the ground they walk on," I admit- 45

ted. "Not the women, you understand, just the ground they walk on. For example," I said, and fished out a locket encircling my throat that contained a few grains of sand, "Marlene Dietrich trod over this bit of Morocco, in the film of the same name, while pursuing Gary Cooper. In my forty-room penthouse in New York, I have a unique collection of other kinds of dirt collected from Louella Parsons, Sheilah Graham, and Joyce Haber—all certified by dealers."

"To think they have dealers for such things in America," she said in disgust. "You make my hair stand on end."

"Really?" I said eagerly. "Wait till you hear about our orgies—"

"I have read accounts," she snapped, and arose. "The tour is now starting. To the bus, everybody!" she called. "Take your cameras, and remember to wear your insignia. Do you people have all your buttons?"

It was painfully evident to me that a number of them did not—were, in fact, in their second childhood—but despite premonitions that I had fallen among feebs, I tagged along.

The forebodings proved groundless; my companions turned out to be alert, well-informed folk—Scientologists and members of the John Birch Society, readers of Ayn Rand, Victor Riesel, and William Buckley, thoroughly immunized against any Bolshevist propaganda. Many, nevertheless, paled visibly on entering the Kremlin walls, and at each reference of Natasha to V. I. Lenin and his achievements, crossed their fingers and murmured the name of Ronald Reagan. There followed a brief, tantalizing peep at the thrones of the Tsars, the imperial carriages, and the jeweled knickknacks of M. Fabergé. We were then whisked through several dank churches to equate our melancholia with that of the populace—a traditional Russian form of welcome—and were hustled back to the Pectopah for lunch.

I shared the meal of waterlogged borscht, herrings in peanut oil, and apricot flan with an Indiana couple and a short, bearded gentleman from Far Rockaway. Mrs. Ziegler, concealed behind dark shades, was a hair freak, obsessed with her coiffure. She kept complaining that the hotel had no beauty parlor (untrue) and that she looked a mess (incontestable). Her mate, a hardware dealer, wore a perpetual frozen grin. You knew, as did he, that she was on borrowed time; the only imponderable was how he would beat the murder rap. I figured he would dissolve flypaper rolls in their soup, which leaves no trace. Mr. Seymour Jasmine, though, perplexed me. The carefully combed white Vandyke and manicured hands bespoke a proctologist retired on Social Security. To my surprise, he revealed himself as an artist specializing in calendars.

"Strictly in the tradition of the Old Masters—Maxfield Parrish, Howard Chandler Christy," he said with an Olympian wave. "I don't believe in this modern dreck, dripping paint on the picture, two eyes on one side of the nose. Now you take a genius like Norman Rockwell. Shall I tell you something? When he paints a little tot eating cherries, birds fly down and peck the fruit off the canvas."

Bemused by a vision of Rockwell fending off such kamikaze attacks, I failed to notice the approach of Natasha with a thunderbolt. It emerged that owing to a shortage of beds in the hotel, Jasmine and I would have to double up. "Just temporary, until we fly to Kiev," she explained, "but two artistic people, I know you will be happy together."

Our honeymoon began inauspiciously. Returning to the room at dusk, I came upon Jasmine stretched out like a flounder, beard disheveled and groaning distractedly. "I'm dying," he gasped. "It's the herring we ate—peanut oil never agrees with me. My wife would kill me if she ever found out."

"Boy, are you in a spot," I sympathized. "Even if you survive the herring there'll always be the threat of your wife. Well, I won't breathe a word."

He stared at me round-eyed. "How could you? She's in Far Rockaway."

"What are we conducting—a course in logic?" I asked sharply. "I thought you were dying. Do you want a priest?"

"A priest?" Jasmine reared up wildly. "You mistook me for a Gentile? Maybe my wife and I don't attend synagogue—"

"Will you for God's sake quit harping on your wife?" I rasped. "I'm sick of her." It had finally dawned on me from my premedical training a few decades back that the man was too feverish to think straight. "Listen, can you hear me?" I shouted into his ear. "Whatever happens, remain in the horizontal, avoid coitus and all fatty foods, and restrict your water intake. I'll get help, but I may have to pull wires."

By also pulling my hair, I made our dragon of a concierge understand the emergency, and an impassive woman doctor shortly materialized, armed with obstetrical clamps and a hypodermic needle large enough to dope a racehorse. By the time a translator, half the staff, and divers passersby had crowded in, the place resembled the stateroom in *A Night at the Opera*. Jasmine's intestinal secrets were plumbed as carefully as though he had been caught smuggling diamonds out of the Rand. Once his nail parings had been filed in envelopes, however, the doctor produced a white powder called Reztlesakla that he took with misgivings. He complained it did no good, but when I showed him it was Alka-Seltzer spelt backward, he quieted down and slept like a baby.

By an odd coincidence, I too was stricken, though quite differently, in our final days in Moscow. As a result of being dragged through too many monasteries, I absorbed more sacred enamel than my system could tolerate and came down with icon poisoning. The American press corps rendered invaluable assistance in this extremity. They referred me to a beautiful Russian ophthalmologist who advised smoked glasses and isolation in my room (I *think* she said mine rather than hers; the words are identical in Russian). "You must never look at another icon," she warned. "Also, moderation in blinis made of flannel." In the event, the distemper vanished as suddenly as it had come, but regrettably, so did the ravishing Dr. Vassileyev.

Within hours of arrival at Kiev, the capital of the Ukraine, I received a tribute that put roses in my cheeks: my suitcase was jimmied open and two cambric handkerchiefs removed. That the KGB felt me sufficiently important to subject my linen to cryptographic analysis turned my head, and I rather tended to patronize the rest of the tour as squares. Mulling it over later, though, I realized my theory was erroneous. The secret police were hardly such bunglers as to have broken the lock; it was, therefore, an inside job. To get even with a Russian hotel whose food is unspeakable, to say nothing of its language, requires cunning, but I succeeded. Thenceforth I never purchased a single postcard of astronauts. That's where it hurts them—in the pocketbook.

Our flock departed Kiev with a kaleidoscope of memories—a hydrofoil ride on the River Dnieper, a plethora of heroic statuary ablaze with bronze radiator paint, and endless shuffling through basilicas, the last of no value except to participants in an ecumenical conference. The one civic statistic I retained was that the city had been founded in A.D. 860 by Yaroslav the Wise, whose two sons, unless my ears deceived me, were Yaroslav the Dolt and Yaroslav the Noodge. En route to the airport we were rigorously checked, and those lacking wooden humpty-dumpties, tin jewelry, toy balalaikas, and Ukrainian blouses were penalized and herded into foreign-currency stores. It was a colorful band indeed, in babushkas and sleazy Cossack caps, that boarded the Aeroflot flight to Simferopol and the Crimea. We could easily have passed for gypsies pinched in a raid on a Sixth Avenue palmistry grift.

Why anyone who has seen Miami or Atlantic City should voluntarily allow himself to be keelhauled through the grueling excursion by air and coach to Yalta defies the understanding. There is, admittedly, one site of historic interest, the chamber where Roosevelt, Churchill, and Stalin confered in 1944. Otherwise, Yalta contains sanitariums that ignite more hypochondria in the onlooker than *The Magic Mountain,* a loony Mauro-Tudor castle, and the paltriest beach outside southwest England. That Chekhov managed to glean any literary nuggets from Yalta is merely added proof of his stature. Happily, after a vain search of the boardwalk for saltwater taffy and two days of being giggled at by the brawny, we were sprung.

Fabled Leningrad, the St. Petersburg of the Winter Palace and the Nevsky Prospekt, of Catherine II and Rasputin, the cradle of the Revolution and so many novels, was our next and final stop, and the group bubbled with expectation.

The grand old city did not let us down. What if, despite all the chauvinistic flapdoodle about Russian architecture, those magnificent structures bordering the Neva were the handiwork of

Italians like Rastrelli? It was all the more an intoxicating vista, a triumph of the serene and classical eighteenth-century style. What if the city's tap water was lethal, so polluted that scores would be felled by giardiasis on their return home? They would have seen the incomparable Hermitage Museum and could upstage their friends who had not—which is, after all, Joe Blow's chief motivation for travel. Several of the party, in fact, had already become such authorities on Russia that they were disputing the Intourist guide. This reached its apogee at Petrodvorets, the founding monarch's castle on the Gulf of Finland.

"If Peter the Great was six feet seven, as you claim," Seymour Jasmine quizzed our cicerone with Talmudic subtlety, "how could he walk in a room with such low ceilings?" Before the girl could reply, he seized the baton. "The answer is, they called him great because he was a genius. Physically he was a man about my size."

"You're crazy," spoke up a Mrs. Feldspar from Altoona. "He was a giant—you're a shrimp. I bet you're not over five foot four."

Jasmine's beard fairly bristled. "For your information, madam, I am five feet five," he said icily. "And I'll tell you something. A lot of very famous people were medium size. Napoleon. Billy Rose. Mervyn LeRoy. Abraham Beame."

"I never heard of that last one," she retorted. "You made him up."

"Nobody could make up Beame," I put in. "You'd need a jeweler's loupe."

"You stay out of this!" Jasmine snarled, and whirled on the lady. "Abe Beame is a living person—my own uncle circumcised him. Are you calling me a liar?"

Bystanders intervened, and satisfaction was obtained without resorting to the code duello. Weary of acrimony at this juncture, I decided to get a view of Leningrad more to my taste. I did so through the eyes of a friend whose eyes, inarguably, are unsurpassed.

Miss Elizabeth Taylor was filming *The Bluebird*, a joint Russo-American production based on Maeterlinck's play and directed by George Cukor. The warehouse the studio occupied somehow brought to mind those sinister cobwebbed godowns in Limehouse Reach prowled by Dr. Fu-Manchu. Elizabeth, impersonating a fairy godmother, was dressed fit to kill in clouds of white chiffon sewn with pearls. She wore a sparkly tiara with wand to match and bore herself through fourteen takes with stoic calm—her Russian leading man, coincidentally, happened to be named Stoic Colm—and altogether looked so delectable that I voted her Queen of the Prom.

"Christmas, my feet hurt," she sighed as we sat in her hotel suite later sipping French 75's. "Not from work—from inactivity. Do you know, I've been here four months and that two-minute scene we just shot is the first one we've printed."

"How is the money?"

"It's good but it's small," she said. "Fifteen rubles a day, and the muzzlers don't even give you carfare."

"You're pulling my leg."

"Scout's honor. This is Russia, buster—everybody here works for scale, and it's murder. When I finish paying for the laundry, a manicure, a couple of pairs of stockings, there's nothing left. A girl can't get very far on fifteen rubles a day."

"Yes, but you have lots of beaux. Any live ones around?"

"In this town? They roll up the canals every night at nine. A commissar took me to a symposium on Friedrich Engels, blew me to a dish of salted cucumbers, and made me walk home." She stared down moodily at the cruiser *Aurora*, the ship on which the Revolution was born, riding at anchor on the Neva. "Still, I suppose it's better to be working than hanging around a ski tow in Klosters with a bunch of vapid millionaires."

I had to admire her pluck. "Right, and who knows? Maybe some Hollywood exec will catch you in this pic and give you a real break. In the meanwhile," I said, rising and extracting my billfold, "how about a few simoleons to tide you over?"

"No, honey, I couldn't." A tear dimmed her dazzling blue orbs. "You've been a darling, but I'll make out somehow. Goodbye, and have a wonderful, wonderful trip wherever you roam."

Goldurn, I told myself as I joined my tour's farewell gala in the Pectopah afterward, if these plutocrats with their paper hats and noisemakers could only see that lonely little figure up there. Pampered Americans, they had so much and she had so little. They had herrings in peanut oil and little torpedoes fried in deep fat, and they were going to have acidosis and giardiasis and everything the world hungered for. And she? Well, she was due on the set next morning with hair done, in full makeup and lines letter-perfect, else she might even be denied those fifteen lousy rubles. It was a dramatic exposition of the difference between two opposing political systems, and I felt privileged to have witnessed it. I drank a glass of plain seltzer, made the rounds of the company to estimate the mathematical odds that our paths would ever cross again, and buoyant at the outcome, skipped upstairs to pack.

4

The Nearer the East,
the Shorter the Shrift

The two young Turks manning the tourist booth in Istanbul's Yesilköy Airport stood aghast as I stripped off my jacket and necktie, removed my belt, and loosened the zipper catch of my trousers. "Pray give me your undivided, gentlemen," I commanded them. "For the last two hours, ever since my flight arrived from Moscow, I have been desperately trying to focus your attention on my problem, one that you seem incapable of grappling with. Actually, this should occasion no surprise; tests recently made here by a team of unprejudiced Greek psychologists indicate that you fellows have the shortest attention span of any race in Europe or Asia. The slightest distraction—a fly buzzing past, a steamboat whistle, a pretty girl's ankle—so destroys your power of concentration that nothing short of a cattle prod can arouse you. Obviously, then, one can only dispel your stupor by some dramatic gesture. Five seconds hence, I shall stand here in my birthday suit, naked, nude, bareass—do you follow me?—which will result in my arrest, thereby forcing the American Ambassador to intercede in my behalf, and creating such a scandal that both of you will be discharged, strangled with a bowstring, placed in silken bags weighted with stones, and sunk to the floor of the Bosphorus. Is that what you want? O.K., here goes—"

"Please listen, *Geheimrat!*" one of them pleaded, apparently hoping the German honorific would deter me. "Since you did not show up yesterday, your passage aboard the S.S. *Iskanderun* was canceled!"

"Stuff and nonsense. I have a letter from your Minister of Tourism, signed in his own blood, promising to hold my cabin."

"The Minister of Tourism resigned last Tuesday owing to dust in his pancreas. He has gone to Switzerland for treatment."

"Then call up his successor. Tell him diplomatic relations between our countries will be suspended unless I sail for the Aegean on Friday."

"His successor is absent from the office today. His wife is in labor with three obstetricians in attendance. The baby is transversed."

"Then call up the Turkish Maritime Lines. I paid for that goddam ticket four months ago—"

"We *have* been calling but their own telephone is busy. After all, Istanbul is not like your Chicago or Detroit where they have many phones."

I know a stone wall when I see it, and that one was as insurmountable as the south wall of Nandi Parva; my projected voyage around the southern periphery of Turkey, which had entailed endless correspondence and cables, was stalled, if not indeed doomed. There was, clearly, but one recourse left to me—to park in Istanbul and harass the steamship line, which I proceeded to do.

The portents were disquieting. Frogmen had discovered a leak in the S.S. *Iskanderun*—or perhaps in its captain, my knowledge of Turkish was rudimentary—and marine urologists doubted if either could be made seaworthy by departure time. Her sister ship, the *Ankara*, had been pressed into service instead, but she was fully booked, though a remote possibility existed that a bed might be installed for me in the chain locker. In this my darkest hour, a fat angel miraculously appeared and with a wave of her wand dispersed the haze of bureaucracy. Roxana, whose plump beauty recalled those massive favorites of the Ottoman sultans, derived a scanty wage as interpreter for the local bureau of Reuter's. I plied her with quantities of Turkish delight and halvah, and in return she winkled out a first-class cabin for me on the *Ankara*. I shall never forget her great mascara-trimmed eyes, awash in carbohydrates, bidding me farewell as we steamed out of the Golden Horn.

My fellow-passengers aboard the *Ankara*—originally a U.S. Coast Guard hospital ship named *Solace* and refitted for the Turkish holiday trade—were pretty much what one would encounter on a Caribbean pleasure cruise, a mixture of businessmen and professionals bound for the resorts dotting the Turquoise Coast. At the outset, mealtimes were a vexation to the spirit, inasmuch as my table companions were baffled by every patois I attempted, including Pushtu, Volapük, Esperanto, and even Lenni-Lenape, the argot the Delaware Indians employed in Bucks County. Wearying at length of sign language, I finally got myself transferred to a group that understood English in varying degree. It including a craggy old civil engineer from Oregon, a young American officer and his family stationed at the NATO base in Izmir, a Turkish lady pediatrician who had interned in the States, and an English schoolmaster. Of these, the latter predictably turned out to be the best value; educated at Cambridge, he had known E. M. Forster and Montague Rhodes James, served in Africa and New Guinea as administrator of the British version of our Peace Corps, and taught history at Winchester.

"I say," I remarked to him, indicating several tablefuls of elderly, affluent people festooned with cameras, light meters, and field glasses, whose dialogue crackled with more explosive gutturals than a Wagnerian opera. "Who in the world are they?"

"Instinct should tell you, my dear chap," he replied. "Those are Teutons hell-bent on Kultur. They're all equipped with Baedekers and archaeological surveys of Ephesus, Pergamum, and Halicarnassus, and as we progress from Izmir to Fethiye, Antalya, Alanya, and Mersin, they will swarm off into a series of Mercedes-Benz buses to gobble up the visibly fake antiques planted there by dealers."

His forecast was correct. Whether it was the Teutons' zeal that put me off, or a relapse of the ecclesiastical virus contracted in too many Russian cathedrals, or the stupefying heat, I had no stomach for Greek amphitheaters, and I decided to confine my sightseeing to the towns. Izmir's seafront, its old-fashioned coastal shipping, cafés, and Victorian facades, were delightful, and the variety of wares in its colorful bazaar outstanding. It was astonishing, by the way, to see how inexpensive the ordinary necessities of life were as compared to those in the States. A first-class broom, such as would cost $2.38 in an American supermarket, retailed here for 82 cents. I was strongly tempted to pick up half a dozen as presents for weekend hosts at home, but the complexities of transporting them in my baggage across Asia dissuaded me.

That much said, however, the rest of Izmir's business area, and those in the other ports, was purgatorial, an affliction and a malaise. The Turks have succumbed to the worldwide infatuation with the motor scooter, recklessly dismembering pedestrians and whizzing at breakneck speed through byways designed for the ox cart. What a satisfying assertion of one's virility it is, as the Italians long ago discovered, to gun these fiendish machines, what more convenient outlet for his xenophobia than to spray some hapless foreigner with mud and watch him dive for cover! My experience in Antalya may well be a classic demonstration. As I stood deafened by the clatter of steam hammers demolishing a kiosk in its main street, two Vespas bore down on me from opposite directions. So close did they pass that they sheared off eight buttons from my sleeves (it was, as the knowledgeable will instantly guess, an English jacket). I naturally shook my fist after them and jumped up and down on my hat like Edgar Kennedy, but it availed me naught.

Each evening, once the bedlam of the ports was left behind, the *Ankara* resumed her way southeastward along a coastline of fantastic beauty. It was undeniable that these magnificent beaches and cliffs, forested by umbrella pines and backed by the spectacular Taurus range, were unique, surpassing even those along the Adriatic coast of Yugoslavia, and yet, as the week wore on, I became conscious of a certain monotony; the rapture engendered by pure scenery, not to say life on shipboard, is subject to the law of diminishing returns. Call me a flibbertigibbet, a man with a grasshopper mind, but by the seventh day of the voyage I was satiated. I was tired of Shredded Wheat saturated with honey and pistachio nuts, sick of the postprandial raki in the bar, fed up with the three-piece combo's rendition of "Ciaou Ciaou Bambina." I was not sorry when the vessel finally dropped anchor off Marmaris, my transfer point to Greece.

Some eighteen miles across the Aegean, or a three-hour ferry ride by caïque, lies the island of Rhodes, where I had spent a month the year before in a villa at Lindos. The charms of that hamlet having been extolled since the pre-Christian era in every guidebook, travel folder, and home movie, there is no need for this troubadour to gild the lily, but it must be admitted that Lindos is addictive. Visitors yearn to get back to the steep huddle of whitewashed dwellings nestled below its acropolis; in wintry northern climes they squirrel away their savings so that they may loll again on its shelving beach encircled by jagged hills and improbable blue water. Some visitors never leave, as witness the small permanent colony of artists and writers; others—notably flaxen-haired English and Scandinavian beauties—are drawn back annually by lust for the bronzed donkey boys who escort trippers aloft to the temple.

My own motive in returning to Lindos was more prosaic. During my previous stay, a tailor named Vlakos had fashioned me a suit of a locally woven white cotton cloth. The finished product, modeled on a garment I had supplied him with, was adequate if a bit snug in the derrière, but once away from the island, a major flaw emerged—the pants pockets were too shallow. Whenever I sat down, paper money, coins, and keys tumbled forth; by a conservative estimate, every time I wore the suit it cost me between sixteen and eighteen dollars in lost currency. I had, therefore, cannily arranged my travel schedule so that I could stop over in Lindos, point out the imperfection to Vlakos, and force him, legally if necessary, to deepen the pockets. After all, I reasoned, the man's professional reputation was at stake. If it were bruited about the Dodecanese that Vlakos suits had shallow pockets, he might well become a pariah in time, and unable to secure clients, ultimately starve. I was too compassionate by nature to drag him through the courts, but on the other hand I knew my rights.

By a happy coincidence, the villa I had occupied earlier, overlooking the harbor, proved to be available, equipped with every amenity including an excellent library. My first couple of days there were sybaritic. I basked on the patio toasting myself a rich golden brown, a copy of the maxims of La Rochefoucauld ostentatiously displayed at my elbow to impress anyone who dropped in. The results fell short of expectation. My only caller was Tapioca, the Greek harridan who rinsed out the towels, and skinwise I turned a glowing ruby color, shading off into rose quartz, of an intensity Renoir had never equaled in his palette. The discomfort might have abated in due course, except that some lemons fell off a tree onto the sunburn, the contusions of which required sulfa drugs. While recovering, I began to hear again the same patter of little feet that had distressed me the year before. Not to put too fine a point on it, the villa was alive with rats. They dwelt in a nest overhead in the bougainvillea, where they had lived since the age of Pericles and consequently regarded me and other tenants as interlopers. Their boldness—or more properly, their hubris, since they were Greek—was on a par with that of the East African hyena. On one occasion, I surprised a group of them bearing away a   *63* tin of Quaker Oats on their shoulders palanquin style. On another, a veritable giant, the size of a small beaver, fell out of the vine nose downward, landing on a marble-topped coffee table. Regaining his wind after a moment, he arose with an air of injured dignity, then deliberately overturned the table in a flash of temper. Nettled by the rodents' contempt for the traps I planted, I resorted to poison and found that they thrived on it—but only on the fresh nuggets wrapped in cellophane. When I sprinkled about the contents of an open, half-used packet, they sniffed the seeds fastidiously and, shuddering like gourmets who had blundered into a Mexican taco shop, stalked off.

As soon as the ravages of sunburn had subsided, I hastened to the plateia, the communal square, in search of Vlakos. The daily tourist influx, apparently, had increased threefold during my absence; eighty busloads of Scandinavians, Germans, Dutch, English, and Americans poured in each morning from Rhodes, with resultant turmoil. New boutiques bloomed in every cranny, all featuring identical embroidery, sandals, and headgear manufactured in Athens; donkeys laden with simpering *Hausfrauen* charged through the cobbled alleys; an unending stream of surfers, picnickers, anglers, and angle-seekers choked the souvenir and grocery shops. Vlakos' tailoring premises, in contrast, showed no glimmer of activity. The windows were boarded up and nobody had a clue to his whereabouts. At last, by intensive sleuthing, I discovered that he had forsworn the needle for a job as scullion in a seaside restaurant. The steam and hubbub in its kitchen, where I found him ladling out goulash and souvlaki from a couple of vast copper drums, made it a somewhat less than ideal setting for our chat, but I had too much at stake to bother with niceties.

"Hi there, Vlakos!" I saluted him jovially. "I see you're dishing it out, so I surmise you can also take it—*n'est-ce pas?* You recall these pants?" I tapped the pair slung over my arm. "Well, I just want you to know that you goofed on the pockets—they're laughable. Did I say laughable? They're a travesty—a bloody farce!"

He scowled at me. "What are you talking to me about pants? I'm the cook here."

Realizing that he had chosen sabers rather than the épée, I followed suit. "Don't try to weasel your way out of it, Clyde," I said roughly. "I've worn pockets from all over the world—Savile Row, Madison Avenue, sweatshops on the East Side, so get this straight. I've worked hard and I've played hard and I've taken my fun where I found it, but by the Almighty, I've yet to see so atrocious a botch, whether in Seattle's Skid Row or the lowest boozing kens of Barcelona. Look!" I exclaimed, spreading open a pocket. "I can barely reach inside—is it any wonder my dough falls out? Answer me, you black-hearted Peloponnesian dog!"

Well, at this, the manager and the chef, who had stood by frozen, started berating Vlakos for soldiering on the job, and the latter, with an angry gesture, snatched up the trousers, rolled them into a ball, and muttered a promise to rectify his handiwork. Four days later he turned up at my door with some cock-and-bull story to the effect that cloth suitable for the repair was no longer in stock. I ordered him to substitute homespun, bed ticking, even denim, but in any event to get a move on, as I was leaving for Israel in seventy-two hours. Having heard nothing by the eve of my departure, I hurried around to the restaurant's kitchen. There, spread-eagled on the floor, lay my trousers, with Vlakos kneeling on them and frantically snipping oblongs out of a ragged pillowcase. From the way his knuckles whitened on the scissors when he caught sight of me, I sensed that I had better keep a civil tongue in my head, and I silently withdrew. Shortly after midnight, an urchin with a knife in his belt delivered my altered trousers, liberally streaked with souvlaki grease, together with a bill for 490 drachmas, or fourteen dollars, which I paid without protest.

Some three weeks afterward, the curator of the Costume Institute at the Metropolitan Museum of Art in New York received a communication from a gentleman traveling in the Middle East. While vacationing in Rhodes, the writer stated, he had come into possession of an article that was, so far as he knew, uncatalogued and sui generis. It was a pair of cotton trousers with graduated pockets, in each case a shallow pouch attached to a deeper one. "The design," he explained, "appears to serve no useful purpose inasmuch as the pockets are sealed off one from the other. I wonder whether the Museum would be interested in acquiring this garment, either by purchase or, if all else fails, as a gift. I enclose a stamped, self-addressed envelope."

The bureaucracy at the Metropolitan Museum of Art, as is well known, is more deeply ingrained than anywhere on earth save Turkey, so it was no wonder I never got a peep out of them; my letter probably went straight into the wastebasket. Well, that's O.K. So did the pants, along with some illusions I had nurtured from youth about the glories of the Turquoise Coast and the Dodecanese. But that too is O.K. If all else fails, I've still got the Aleutians.

5

Unshorn Locks
and Bogus Bagels

Bronzed and wiry, his figure as compactly mus-
cled as a gymnast's, his black eyes asparkle under
a leonine snow-white mane, the Israeli in the
white tunic could have been some world-famous
maestro like Leonard Bernstein wielding his baton on the podium of the Albert Hall. He moved
with the grace and precision of a ballet dancer,
embodying at once the vivacity of Chaplin and the
intensity of Picasso. And as much of an artist in
his own way, I thought, for never in memory had
I beheld such dexterity in a barber. Studying him
in the mirror as he circled about me, I marveled
at the lightning play of scissors over the frisure I
had grown in Russia and Greece. Withal, and despite my reluctance to interfere with genius, past
experience warned that the chap needed guidance. I craned around, narrowly avoiding a stab
in the medulla oblongata.

"Now for God's sake will you trim it low in the

back?" I enjoined him. "I'm not a Polack miner down from Scranton on payday."

He instantly took umbrage—an overdose. "Listen, you think I just graduated barber college? I was cutting hair when you were a kid in *cheder!*"

"I never went to Hebrew school. My folks didn't believe in it."

"You don't have to pretend," he said acidly. "I knew you were a goy the minute you walked in." My disavowal fell on deaf ears. "Look, mister, it's no difference by me what you are—a Jew, an Arab, a Chinaman. All I ask is don't waggle the head in the chair, because one thing drives a barber crazy, it's a customer with Parkinson's. So how long you're in Tel Aviv?"

I replied that I had just skyed in from Athens, yoking it with a civil request not to shave my neck. From the ferocity with which he now addressed it, I feared lest he sever the jugular, but he contented himself with a few trifling contusions. When, however, I flatly refused to let him trim my moustache, his bile boiled over.

"You want an advice from a tonsorial engineer?" he asked. "Nobody's got a *schwanz* like yours any more—it's an antique. Better it should droop around the mouth on both sides. That's how all the swingers wear it now."

"So did Bobby Vernon in those Keystone comedies in 1917," I said. "Well, I get more yocks with it this way. Leave it alone."

"O.K., you're the boss. The hair in the nose and ears—you want I should leave that too? It's so long you look already like a tiger."

"The very endearment my lady friends use," I returned sweetly. "They claim I've got the same kind of virility."

"Hoo ha!" he crowed. "So we got here a sexpot? Well, well, you fooled me. From the liver spots on your chest, I thought you had one foot in the grave." With an insolent flourish, he yanked off my apron. "Shampoo? Massage? Anything on the hair?" Faced with wooden sales resistance, he gestured toward an array of bottles. "How about some real Israeli Chutzpah?"

"The sample you've given me will suffice." I arose in my iciest Sumner Welles manner. "I'll have the check, please, and a minimum of sass."

Though the descent from the barber shop to the lobby of the Tel Aviv Xanadu took but seconds, my huff subsided at the scene confronting me. Allrightniks of every nationality—American, French, German, Scandinavian, Dutch—milled about in gaudy swim attire, muumuus, and terry robes, exchanging banter and fervent embraces, challenges to race in the pool, boasts to vanquish each other at gin rummy and handball. Women as steatopygous as Rose Sydell's Bounteous Belles elbowed me aside, boisterous infants drooled on my shoes, smoke from expensive Havanas stung my eyelids. Hardened cynic though I am, emotion misted over my spectacles. What magic, what ingenuity and manpower it had taken to re-create Grossinger's, the Miami Fontainebleau, and the Concord Hotel on a barren strand in the Near East! Bit by bit I began to comprehend the obstacles, the indomitable will that had wrought this miracle.

Meanwhile, however, a sudden pang of hunger overswept me, coupled with indecision. In which of the Xanadu's tempting facilities ought I feed the inner man? The Golden Matzoh Room, obviously, was designed for gourmets, La Belle Snackereuse for nibblers, and the Sugarfoot Lounge for the sweet of tooth. Providentially, the resident manager of the hotel, Kublai Kahn (nephew of Morris, its founder), had here decreed a Pastrami Pleasure Dome as well as a Herring Haven, and sensing that the former promised more, I made for it apace. "Tip-top New York-style corned beef that melts in the *kishkes!*" trumpeted the menu. "Succulent smoked turkey-and-lingonberry sandwiches, the same as in Gotham's Carnegie Delicatessen!" I salivated like Tommy Manville presented with a virgin of seventeen. When the waiter in the fullness of time set down a plate before me, I gaped at it nonplussed.

"What is this abomination?" I croaked, pointing at the wet poppyseed roll containing two slices of cold gray fat and a fried onion in a bed of camellias.

"So what should it be?" he demanded with the indigenous fondness for answering a question with a question. "It's a hot brisket sandwich like you ordered." He thrust a check and a pencil under my nose. "What's the matter, you don't like?"

"I adore," I said, scrawling my signature.   71

"Wrap it in Kleenex and file it in the nearest cloaca." I stalked out of the hotel, found my way to a pizza parlor, and dined on a can of warmed-over Van Camp's Spaghetti. Then, childishly defiant of the hundred-degree temperature, I struck out along Dizengoff Street, Tel Aviv's main apple, for a survey of the town.

Whatever else Tel Aviv lacked, there was no shortage of cement block. Miles of squat concrete housing alternated with small groceries, fast-food shops, and candy stores; the pedestrians, save for occasional perky Sabras in uniform, were elderly, apathetic, drained by the remorseless humidity and glare. There was no sense of the foreign, nothing evocative of the past—the place was as exotic as suburban Moscow or the antipodes of the Bronx. The Mediterranean littoral, a few streets distant, was fringed by skyscraper hotels, largely incomplete because of inflation and over-confidence in their tourist potential. Beyond them, the city dissolved into an Orwellian nightmare, reminiscent of Flanders Fields, of crumbling walls, shuttered onetime dwellings, and weedy excavations that stetched away to Old Jaffa. To pursue this inspection, at the risk of sunstroke or a possible syncope, was tantamount to filing my will for probate. Availing myself of a fifteen-cent entertainment guide, I took refuge in a nearby café.

Over a dismal milk shake, I thumbed through "This Week in Israel," and presto—the diversion I sought leaped out of its pages: an advertisement for the most extraordinary beauty aid I had ever heard of. Above a photo of a saucy Israeli chick with a Leslie Caron pout blared the legend: "Israel's No. 1 Perfume—Say it with CHUTZPAH . . . it's direct, arrogant, provokingly natural like the Sabras. Chutzpah and Mazel Tov—Israel's renowned perfumes (also colognes and after shaves)." I sat back dumbfounded, doubting the evidence of my eyes. So this was what had greeted me in the hairdressing salon—not just the impertinence of one single barber, but an actual lotion synthesizing cockiness, bluster, contumely—a distillation, in short, of hubris. Could this cologne be what the waiter in the delicatessen reeked of, or was it his own natural offensiveness? Brooding over the phenomenon, something else occurred to me. While Israelis had been the first to compound and package it, theirs was no corner on effrontery. We too overseas had our impudence experts, black belt masters of chutzpah like Henry Kissinger and George Jessel, Norman Mailer and Milton Berle. (I did not include Don Rickles, who I suspected was trying to pass as a Semite.) And what about our New York taxi drivers? And those immortal waiters in Lindy's who used to ask incredulously, "You're eating the pot roast here? Don't touch it—it's poison. Take better a piece of fish." All the same, I reflected, it would be petty to minimize this newest scientific breakthrough—one that Dr. Chaim Weizmann, himself a chemist, would have applauded. Not a soul in history, from Helen of Troy to Helena Rubinstein, had ever thought of pure, unadulterated gall as a cosmetic.

If Tel Aviv provided any other amusement for the wayfarer, I regrettably missed it. I did, fortunately, meet some of its distinguished actors, like Leah Porat, Yossi Yadin, and Assi Dayan, and several writers, among them Chaim Hefer and Dahn Ben-Amotz, all of whom were exceptionally gifted and articulate. They had traveled widely, were multilingual, and were totally devoid of the chauvinism and aggressiveness said to be rife in Israel. With others, I was conscious sometimes of a provincialism, a lack of interest in world problems, difficult to account for in a society of so many racial origins. The excuse advanced, that this was to be expected of people fighting for their preservation, was undoubtedly valid, but indifference and self-absorption, it seemed to me, were traits hardly calculated to win friends and influence tourism.

Whether the pace at the Xanadu was too swift, or because I was afraid I might defenestrate myself if I spent another night there, I bought a seat in a *cheroot* leaving that afternoon for Jerusalem. Rather than a large Burmese cigar, it turned out to be a sedan accommodating seven persons. The one next to me was a recent convert to Judaism named Mr. Graham Greenspan, from Pascagoula, Mississippi. He wore over his shorts a shirt made from a flour bag, a pair of black silk socks, and a conical Tyrolean straw. What made him distinctive, though, was the talisman suspended from a silver chain around his throat—a life-sized ceramic bagel sprinkled with ceramic salt, out of which a bite had presumably been taken.

"I've worn it since I saw the light," he explained proudly. "It's a conversation piece. It tips off my religious affiliation to people—by innuendo, without rubbing their nose in it. Guess where it originated from."

I guessed Riyadh, Saudi Arabia, or possibly the grave of Dr. Goebbels, and was spared the burden of further chitchat. Once in Jerusalem, angels must have been charged with seeing to my welfare, because the hotel I checked into, the American Colony, proved a windfall. The former residence of a Turkish pasha, it had been operated for generations by a Baptist family and was an oasis for foreign journalists—understandably, since it was cool, peaceful, and attractive. The Islamic staff, furthermore, was civil and unobtrusive, well trained by its present manager, a Briton concerned with maintaining a hospitable, old-fashioned tradition. After the brouhaha of the Xanadu, it was a blessing.

Still smarting from my captive tour of Russian churches, I resolved to make this stay in Jerusalem as anticlerical and unorthodox as I could. If it were possible to avoid cathedrals, temples, and mosques, I was going to avoid them. I would flee from every hallowed shrine and chapel, shun as the plague all sanctified tombs and crypts. The moment I made the decision, I panicked, certain that my presumption was about to earn me a bolt of lightning from an enraged Jehovah. Nothing happened; a fly buzzed lazily overhead and somewhere outside I heard the music of a hurdy-gurdy. An inexpressible joy suffused me. I had *done* it—I had got away with it! I was free of the mandate laid on all visitors to the Holy Land to plod through a lot of malodorous sacred masonry in order to make character with Father Flynn or Rabbi Nussbaum back home.

As a consequence, the next two or three days were idyllic. I explored all the ethnic quarters inside the walls of the old city—Christian, Moslem, Jewish, and Armenian—ate dubious food from the stalls and chaffered in the bazaars for objects I neither liked nor needed. I amassed quantities of brasswork, spurious carpets, daggers, filigree, paintings on velvet, and taborets inlaid with mother-of-pearl which, like A. O. Barnabooth in Valéry Larbaud's novel, I deep-sixed ere quitting the country. I drank blackberry tea with a long-time friend, Colonel Moshe Pearlman, a brilliant soldier and chronicler of Israel's past, and was floored by his scholarly exegesis of Groucho Marx's comedy, a subject he was far more knowledgeable about than I. I trudged innumerable miles from the Wadi Al Guz through the pandemonium of Yafo Street to unearth a Hungarian pastry shop where I gorged myself on Dobos tarts and *Schlagobers.* In the sculpture garden of the Israel Museum, I lingered before the statuary from which Billy Rose had gleaned such rich publicity, and shed a tear for Fanny Brice, from whose artistry Miss Streisand had likewise profited. But most satisfying of all was the five-hour session of reminiscence I shared with Isaac Bashevis Singer in the clamant coffee shop of the King David. He confided to me how, as a stripling of fourteen in Poland captivated by the Sherlock Holmes stories, he had tailed a putative malefactor through the streets of their *shtetl,* only to have his quarry, a harmless chicken-flicker, suddenly whirl on and upbraid him. Grown older and wiser, he said, he finally hit upon his true calling. He was going to build a painstaking replica of Captain Nemo's submarine, complete with player piano and five hundred rolls, and cruise the entire twenty thousand leagues charted by Verne's intrepid hero. Luckily for his readers, of whom I am the most devoted, that dream evaporated.

The one concession I made to sightseeing—and one that might have had a fatal outcome but for quick-wittedness—was a trip to Masada, the ancient fortress on the Dead Sea where nine hundred Zealots chose suicide in A.D. 70 to avoid surrender to the Romans. By some fluke, the yeshiva student who drove me there neglected to mention that it was on a plateau 1,300 feet high. The height would have bothered me not at all, as I was a veritable human fly when younger, able to chin myself from a Welsbach mantle in the kitchen that adults couldn't reach. Here, though, it was the unexpected sight, from two miles off as we approached, of a funicular leading up the escarpment that capsized my stomach.

Wrapping my arms around the driver to gain his attention, I bade him to halt instanter.

"We're doing ninety!" he protested. "Better a dinner of herbs without salt than a stalled car!"

"None of your Biblical lip, smartass," I replied. "Who's paying for this tour—you or me?"

"It says on my slip you're to ride the funicular—"

"Paris green I'll drink first!" The realization that I was dealing with a madman also told me that the Misericordia was my sole recourse. "I'm a heart case," I whimpered. "My pipestems are like arteries—you could ask the biggest professors! Moreover, I'm coming from a very sickly family—the Hapsburgs—we bleed if even a fly lights on our nose!" I whipped out my express checks. "What do you want? Money—women—fame? I'll buy you a ticket to Buenos Aires—the girls there are insatiable! I'll get you on television. . . ."

And that did the trick. Unwittingly I had found his Achilles' heel; he played some instrument, I think the hullabaloo, in a rock group calling themselves The Damp Squibs. We stopped in a gas station at Ein Gedi, where I made a fake overseas call to CBS, procuring them an audition and a split week at the Paramus shopping center. All the way back to Jerusalem, he kept excitedly quizzing me about the gold Levi's he would wear and the hostels they'd sleep in. I promised them carte blanche at the Serendipity, a suite in the Olympic Tower. We parted on my undertaking to meet the rest of the group at nine that evening.

By eight I was in a taxi hell-bent for Tel Aviv, and by eleven, aboard an Air France Caravelle streaking toward Iran. The stewardess, who plied me with brandy and tucked in my blanket, was a dead ringer for Catherine Deneuve and exuded the most divine scent. It was, she said, kissing her fingers, a new creation of the high couture, a dressmaker perfume called La Taquine (The Tease).

"What does it do for you, my little?" I queried. "Does it enrage and exacerbate those inhaling it, as another I know of purports to?"

"*Pas du tout*, monsieur," she said, eyes widening. "The chic types on our *appareil* can barely keep their hands off me. On this Athens-Bombay run, one usually receives three proposals a night"—she sighed happily—"not a single of them decent. Why do you ask?"

"Because I'm raising your average, delectable one," I responded, pinching in all directions. The slap I received was playful, sisterly, a caress more than a rebuff. It gently curbed my coltishness and eased me into slumberland, where chutzpah ceases irking and where carpers cease from carping—but only if every Sabra teases, every sandwich pleases, and barbers deign to smile.

6

The Vintner Buys
the Rolls Nobody Eats

At three o'clock one morning in late July, the residents of Tehran, the Middle East's newest Klondike, lay inert on their rooftops, stoned out of their minds by the fiercest heat wave in fifty years and dreading the approach of another dawn. Sixty-nine persons, said the press, had attempted suicide in the past forty-eight hours—without, curiously, a single fatality. It was a foregone conclusion, hence, that an Aquarian born on the cusp of Snafu with a genius for wrong timing should have chosen that exact moment to arrive in Iran. An airport taxi had just off-loaded my fifty kilos of luggage into the courtyard of a fleabag called the Grand Vizier Hotel and vanished into the haze of pollution. As I staggered heavy-laden into the foyer, buffeted by a blast of arctic air as from a frozen food locker, half a dozen somnolent figures reared up from their armchairs, belligerently clutching their attaché cases. The clerk behind the reception desk, an unshaven brigand sporting a single gold collar button, bolted to his feet, his face contorted like a demon's in a Japanese print.

"Out, out!" he shouted irascibly. "Everything full—no rooms till 1978!"

While this was not quite the rosewater and iced sherbet promised in a hasty update of Omar Khayyám aboard the plane, I was undismayed, having been briefed on the crunch well beforehand. With droves of foreign concessionaires and hustlers pouring into Tehran on every flight, beds were reputedly scarcer than hen's teeth; travelers were shelling out fortunes to doss down in hotel corridors, checkrooms, even shower stalls. Luckily, there was one recourse—baksheesh. I advanced on the desk with a toothy smile more saccharine than Don Ameche in a kiddie pageant.

"Good morning, son," I boomed, jauntily extending one of five business cards prepared in Jerusalem. "J. Rufus Wallingford of the Golconda Kerosene Corporation. I believe my associate Blackie Daw, the saxophone virtuoso, confirmed my reservation—right?" Seizing the clerk's hairy paw, I pressed a crisp century note into it.

"What is this?" he demanded, staring into his palm. "What are you handing me here?"

"Why, just a bit of lolly, my boy." I flicked an infinitesimal speck of ash from his lapel. "A gentle lubricant to oil the wheels of commerce."

"A *bribe?*" he sputtered. "I want you to know I'm an honest man—I don't accept bribes under the counter!" So extreme was his outrage that the entire lobby stiffened to attention. "Put it on *top* of the counter where everyone can see it."

I complied, and with the speed of a mamba striking, his hand shot out, enfolded the bill, and stowed it in his breast. "Welcome to Persia, effendi," he purred, tapping a bell. "Room 417— $66 a day, 22 percent service, and 19 percent surtax if using more than one towel daily."

Later that morning, rejuvenated by five hours of slumber on a bedspring that tattooed waffles all over my *Sitzfleisch,* I ordered up the continental breakfast, poured it down the drain, and made several calls to Iranians recommended by friends. Unhappily, it being the Muslim Sabbath, everyone with wheels had fled to the Caspian beaches for relief. Sooner than moon around a lobby clangorous with Kraut geologists guffawing over their adventures in the Reeperbahn, I went out for a constitutional.

It was a terrifying experience. The Takht-e-Jamshid, the avenue on which the Grand Vizier fronted, is unquestionably and *hors-concours* the world's most demented thoroughfare. A gigantic torrent of buses, lorries, taxis, and motorbikes roars at Mach II speed through a canyon lined with more fly-by-night banks and phony brokerage houses than Wilshire Boulevard's Miracle Mile. The zebras at infrequent intervals are purely ornamental; they act on the Iranian motorist like adrenaline, spurring him to accelerate, and anyone foolhardy enough to cross is guaranteed to wake up in traction. As a result, there are only two kinds of pedestrians in Tehran—the quick and the dead. At almost every intersection, in fact, hordes of layabouts can be witnessed gambling on the accident pools—the highest score of lacerations, fractures, and concussions achieved that day by the scorchers of the Tahkt-e-Jamshid.

Convinced after another sortie or two that Tehran's din and physical ugliness were as appalling as informants had told me, I decided to forgo its spiritual aspects until after I had seen more of the country, and bought myself a three-day tour of the interior. I was met at the airport in Shiraz by a wizened creature in black who introduced himself as Mahmoud, my guide, and the chauffeur of his car, a corpulent Bengali, as Mr. Dodgson. Our first objective was Iran's renowned archaeological site, Persepolis, and en route, succumbing to curiosity, I asked the driver if he were related to Charles Lutwidge Dodgson, the pseudonymous author of *Alice's Adventures in Wonderland*.

"Goodness me, yis, I am remembering old Charlie like yesterday," he chuckled. "That chap my grandfather. Very fine person, oh, yis."

"But he passed away before your time, my friend. He was a contemporary of Queen Victoria."

"Balderdash, sir, I am knowing this man backwards and forwards. A very tiny fellow with smug nose and chin-whisker, always wearing striped pajama coat over his loincloth."

Unable to recall Lewis Carroll possessing any such props, I tried another tack. "What do you make of his predilection for little girls, Mr. Dodgson?" I asked. "In the light of modern psychiatry, 83 wouldn't it seem your ancestor was a bit of a weirdo?"

"Oh, yis, yis—very fine weirdo," he agreed. "But I don't think he live very long after that. My uncle say he was eaten by dogs."

At that juncture, it began to dawn on me that one of us was in a time warp, and I occupied the balance of the trip studying his driving and twisting my prayer beads. I have on occasion been quoted as saying that a chimpanzee can operate a motorcar better than the average Indian. This is a downright calumny. What I said was just the reverse—that driverwise, the average Indian was superior to a chimpanzee. But as has been said of all generalizations, including this one, mine was probably false.

The emotional impact of Persepolis, to put it mildly, boggled the mind; the scale and perfection of the awesome monument reared by Cyrus, Xerxes, and Darius to commemorate their dynasties inevitably ranks it among antiquities like Baalbek and Leptis Magna, and wandering through it, I became steeped in profundities. What comparable relic, I speculated, had such modern satraps as J. P. Morgan, Sewell Avery, and William Randolph Hearst left behind for posterity to cherish? Centuries hence, would some traveler in an antique land gaze upon two vast and pitiless eyes of stone and weep to recall Louis B. Mayer, King of Kings? Unfortunately, my reverie was interrupted time and again by Mahmoud, the guide, as exasperating a nudnick as ever abraded an eardrum. Every doorway, every architrave summoned up the name of celebrities he had escorted around Persepolis—defunct viceroys, Ruritanian noblesse, Midwestern utility tycoons. The list was longer than Burke's Peerage, the voice more strident than an emery wheel. Halfway through his eulogium of some Hungarian boyar, I abruptly tied off his vocal tubes and consigned us back to Shiraz.

As if to compensate, an enchanting treat awaited me; at lunch in the coffee shop of the Hotel Cyrus, I stumbled on one of the great comedy acts of all time—a troupe of waiters whose antics topped anything ever seen in vaudeville or music hall. They were five in number, all squat, shock-haired, and clad in voluminous black coats, their skins glistening with prime Iranian oil and eyes rolling wildly. Their pratfalls were masterly, light years beyond those of the Ritz Brothers. With a crash of trays, cutlery, and glassware, they fell into the dining room through swing doors, ripping off tablecloths and overturning sugar bowls in anxiety to serve the clientele. Exits and entrances were so expertly timed that the performers collided on the split second, invariably spraying onlookers with soup or coffee. Moreover, unlike the Three Stooges' shtick of poking fingers into one another's eyes, these merely maimed themselves, whimpering plaintively as a spoon or fork found its way into their nostrils. They were, in a word, irresistible, but their most brilliant—and thoroughly impromptu—routine was still to come.

It began with a neighboring diner's alarmed

discovery of a roach on the curtain overhanging his table. The waiter he summoned folded a newspaper and struck at the insect, precipitating a shower of dust on his food. Ignoring the guest's outcries, the waiter placed a foot in his groin, mounted, and tried to squash the roach in a napkin. Whereupon the curtain rod tore loose and the two of them, enveloped in a cyclonic bundle that annihilated food and tableware, crashed heavily to the floor. With artistry like that, no real theatergoer sits on his hands. I leaped up and applauded the pair to the echo.

The choice offered me the following morning, of two mausoleums or a circuit of the bazaars, was no contest, and I quickly opted for the latter. It is extraordinary how the childish mind clings to delusions. One pushes his way into endless stifling coulisses, contracting fleas—if not bacilli that could cripple him for life—confident that somewhere in these noisome stalls lie the undiscovered idol's eye, the jade nose-flute sought by curators the world over. The corollary of which, lovingly fostered by tourist handbooks, is that the merchant is a simpleton who can be euchred out of his caftan by hard bargaining. True to form, the unspeakable Mahmoud immediately conducted me to a bunch of rug emporiums he was in league with, and his theatrics when I spat out the hook would have turned Thomashevsky, the eminent Jewish tragedian, green with envy. As a farewell token at the airport, he tendered me an aphrodisiac powder claimed to produce wondrous effect on the male libido. I fed a spoonful to a friend's rooster in Java subsequently and the luckless fowl exploded in midair before our very eyes.

If Isfahan, the ensuing stop on the tour and heralded as its aesthetic climax, disappointed me initially, I soon discovered the reason. Shah Abbas the Great, who built it as his capital in the sixteenth century, had been recompensed not long before by attaching his name to a hotel of such consummate kitsch as to beggar description. Its pretentious decor, a melange of Turkish, Edwardian, Biedermeier, and modernique, matched only by the bumbling inefficiency of its management, prejudiced me before I had a glimpse of the city's palaces and tabernacles. Once I did, the Sheikh-Luftullah and the Shah's Mosques proved an immensely moving experience, and I was especially charmed by the Armenian cathedral in Julfa and the adjacent museum. It was, however, in the Chehel Sotoun, the so-called Palace of Forty Columns, that I passed my most satisfying afternoon. The gardens are a delight to the spirit, extending tranquillity of a kind too seldom found these days. Within the iwan, the small Safavid murals, which are ascribed to an unknown Persian inspired by European engravings, betray Mongol influence as well, and it is absorbing to see how the cross-fertilization of cultures ultimately culminates in a work of art. Altogether, by the time I had had this brief taste of Isfahan's treasures, I was nearly tempted to endure another night at the hotel to sip further, but common sense prevailed over

Kultur, and I caught the last plane back to Tehran.

Though the city hadn't changed in my absence, my luck had; the individuals I had vainly tracked were back in town, and I was received with truly heartwarming friendliness. One couple in particular, a professor of political science and his wife, did everything possible to give me an insight into Persian family life. I shared their meals, helped them dispose of a surplus of liquor at parties that could have been calamitous, and was even present at the adoption of a daughter, a four-day-old foundling. As with many of their friends, people of the professional class, they had been educated in the West and felt a strong kinship with it. Increasingly I began to notice the strong distinction they drew between their Persian heritage and Tehran's explosive boom-town fever. They saw the past being swept away by a frenzied adoration of wealth and personal display, a longing for quadraphonic tape decks, wife swapping, and finger-licking chicken. And their forebodings were indeed valid, nowhere better exemplified than in the Dantesque inferno of traffic and pollution fouling the Takht-e-Jamshid.

The last day of my sojourn, I visited, at my host's insistence, two of Tehran's showplaces—the Archaeological Museum and the Crown Jewels Treasury—which, by an odd coincidence, portrayed the dichotomy in present-day Iran. Perhaps the juxtaposition was deliberate, perhaps not, but it seemed to me significant. Said to be the finest repository of Persian art in the world, the Museum exhibits a fabulous collection of pre-Islamic pottery, Luristan bronzes, statuary from Persepolis, Sasanian mosaics and silver, and miniatures. The objects in the Crown Jewels Treasury, on the other hand, fill a 52-page booklet; included in the gallimaufry are three gem-encrusted thrones, a golden globe weighing eighty pounds set with 51,366 precious stones, a 182-carat pink diamond, an emerald the size of a bar of soap, and countless basins, flasks, dish covers, and hubble-bubbles set with bijoux. All of it reposes in the Central Bank of Iran as security for government obligations and part of the cover for its note issue. The contrast between the two hoards of riches was inescapable. The first represented the incalculable achievement of Persia's most gifted artists and craftsmen; the second, apart from the viscous black gold bubbling out of the nation's crust, was the schlock that upholds modern Iran.

"And where do you go from here, may I ask?" a guest inquired of me at the farewell dinner tendered by my friends.

I replied that much as I had always longed to see Kashmir, the tantrums Madam Gandhi was indulging in and the muzzle she had put on foreign journalists were forcing me to overfly India. "It's rough on my New York acquaintances," I admitted, "but I'll be back there before they expect me."

"Ah, New York!" The man's face became radiant. "How I miss that city! I was a law student there for four years, and I still dream of it. Tell me," he went on, "do you know a section there named Gramercy Park, below Grand Central Station?"

"Yes, as it happens I live there."

"Do you hear that, everybody?" he cried out jubilantly to the group. "At last I've met someone from Gramercy Park! You see," he explained, turning to me, "every so often, when I was in Manhattan, I used to hear commercials on the radio for a tailoring firm called the Gramercy Park Clothiers, and the name haunts me." Tears welled up in his eyes. "The Gramercy Park Clothiers—to this day that spells New York to me, Central Park, those glorious secretaries on Madison Avenue, the Plaza, the Fifth Avenue buses, Greenwich Village . . ."

And that was the memory I carried away from Persia, of a stranger fired to nostalgia by the name of a cut-rate clothing firm. It was trifling, but it set in motion a disturbing train of thought. Samarkand and Timbuctoo were mere names too, but what wild adventure and intolerable privations they had occasioned romantics obsessed with them. Was it possible, for instance, that my own dreams of Kashmir had equally prosaic sources—the sight of a luxurious woolen jacket in Sulka's or some nasal tenor's rendition of the "Kashmiri Love Song"? After all, I remembered sheepishly, I had once ventured all the way to far-off Lamu in Kenya upon hearing of a brothel there called the Eskimo Pie. . . . Well, far better not to probe too deeply into the motives propelling me onward, or I'd be back even sooner in fabled Gramercy Park, the home of the two-pants suit ("Walk up three flights and save 40 percent"). I clenched my knapsack, slung my teeth over my shoulder, and went pensively upstairs into the belly of the big silver bird.

7

Rosy and Sleazy, or Dream and Reality in Asia

If Phee Line Miaow, the Siamese room boy crouched outside a chamber in Bangkok's Oriental Hotel one sweltering afternoon last August, seemed more woebegone than usual, he had reason. Fortnightly on his day off, he was wont to frolic with a certain roly-poly trainee in a massage parlor on Suriwongse Road who furnished him with cut-rate therapy in her spare time. Today, however, owing to a shortage of hotel staff, he had been kept on duty and assigned an extra burden—four deluxe suites honoring Joseph Conrad, Somerset Maugham, Noel Coward, and an unidentified belletrist named (sic) James Mitchener. And as if that were not tribulation enough, they had now saddled him with some lunatic in Room 16, a florid, apoplectic septuagenarian with granny glasses and a cavalry moustache gone to seed. Each time Phee Line had tried the door, seeking to vacuum and change the sheets, the sole response was a protracted groan as of a soul in torment. Unless Number 16 was breathing his last, the youth decided, he must be drunk or freaked out on nose-candy. In whatever case, the devil with him—there was no explaining the behavior of these *farangs*. Enclasping his knees, he gave himself up to fantasies involving his zestful little breastful at the Thousand Delights Massage Parlor.

Actually, Phee Line was mistaken about the sorely beset foreigner, whose visage, as the astute will have guessed, adorned my passport. I had, in strict confidence, taken a nip or two to ward off snakebite, but body and brain were as normal and lucid as those of a child of five. I was merely lying on the floor—the bed having floated out the window sometime earlier—pondering my long connection with Bangkok and mourning its decline. Here, as with Tehran, was yet another monument to Western progress; in three short decades, the sleepy riverine capital of the Thai, whose tree-lined klongs, fanciful wats, and amiable citizenry had so captivated me in 1947 and thereafter, was now become a dizzying megalopolis ablaze with neon, a pestilence of traffic jams, bars, brothels, nightclubs, and allied tourist deadfalls that set the nerves jangling like a vibraharp. Perhaps what underlay my melancholy, though, was an inexplicable disquiet, a conviction that some profound Buddhist truth here, some principle that might have altered my life, had escaped me. Somerset Maugham, describing his sojourn in Bangkok forty years before in *The Gentleman in the Parlour,* had felt the same mixture of repugnance and frustration:

> It is impossible to consider these populous cities of the East without a certain malaise. They are all alike, with their straight streets, their arcades, their tramways, their dust, their blinding sun, their teeming Chinese, their dense traffic, their ceaseless din. They have no history and no tradition. . . . They are hard and glittering and as unreal as the backcloth of a musical comedy. They give you nothing. But when you leave them it is with a feeling that you have missed something and you cannot help thinking that they have some secret that they have kept from you.

Well, I reflected, struggling up from the horizontal, my week in this gigantic ulcer machine was terminating tonight, but prior to leaving, maybe I could elicit one secret at least that dealt, coincidentally, with Maugham himself. I broached the problem to the Eurasian assistant manager, Mr. Almondize, as he was computing my bill.

"This leaflet I found in the desk blotter puzzles me," I said. "It says that Somerset Maugham was so impressed by the hotel that he used it as the setting of his story, *Gentleman in the Parlour.*"

His treacly smile faded, replaced by the hauteur hotelmen betray when their guests behave other than as sheep. "What puzzles you?"

"Why, its blatant distortion of fact," I said. "For one thing, the book isn't a romance or fiction at all—it's a travel diary. For another,

Maugham's description of these premises borders on the vitriolic. He was stricken with malaria here and they begrudged him the space."

"I know nothing about that," he snapped, blowing himself up like a turkey cock. "And besides, I hardly see why it concerns you."

"On the contrary, it very much does," I said. "Since the author in question is too dead to squawk, this friend and admirer feels constrained to. Sweet are the uses of publicity, honey-bun, but let's not forget the good old axiom about truth in advertising. Put that in your opium pipe and smoke it."

Nothing tones up a volcano like blowing off a little lava, and quite reconciled to be deemed a pepper pot, I emplaned for Malaysia purged and refreshed. Nearing my initial stop, Penang, I harked back to the six weeks I had once spent there at the E. & O. Hotel waiting for a vessel to Bombay. Crazed with loneliness, battling ants that threatened the hoard of butterscotch and chocolate creams that buffered me against suicide, I had nevertheless developed a fondness for the place. Its ancient residences and go-downs, the dockside bustle and the jumble of races thronging the streets, typified for me the magic of Kipling's Far East, and I wondered if that image was still valid. Circuiting the town in a pedicab, I discovered its quality had not dimmed. The handsome government buildings, a legacy from Dutch and British rule, had been faithfully restored, and the surrounding trees and gardens exuded a calm and stability that gladdened the heart. Even though a few hotels had sprung up, and the Chinese quarter was swollen beyond recognition, Penang retained the charm of its historic past. Further reassurance awaited me at the old E. & O. Hotel. The same ceiling fans revolved languidly in the rooms, the same dignified elderly Chinese arrived with afternoon tea of potted-meat sandwiches and finger bananas, the same horse-faced spinster in flowered chiffon sat in the lounge reading Jane Austen's *Mansfield Park*. Long will I cherish the week I lay supine on the hotel esplanade gorging myself on candied cherries and watching the clouds mass over the Bay of Bengal. What mattered it if there was no balm in Gilead? I found oodles in Penang.

Strong as the impulse was to tarry and inflate myself to the girth of Tony Galento, the heat of mid-August was stronger, and I finally bowed to British colonial tradition and took to the hills. Cameron Highlands, five thousand feet above the burning coastal plain, turned out to be the kind of retreat I thought existed only in the rhapsodies of travel agents. The air was bracing, the scenery spectacular, the vegetation, a mixture of tropical and mountain foliage, lush and sparkling. (My very first Martini, significantly, was gin supplied by a well-known firm of vintners in Kuala Lumpur, Lush & Sparkling Ltd.) You awoke mornings with a sense of euphoria so acute it was scary—you had to pinch yourself to see if it was real. Unluckily, that was the knock; there was nobody else to pinch. My hotel teemed with exquisite

Malaysian ladies all accompanied by husbands

trained from babyhood to wield a kris—a word closely associated with another Malay term, "to run amok"—and superstitious peasant that I am, I kept my hands at parade rest lest I wind up like a chicken in parts. Thanks to repeated cold showers, however, plus a dish called fried mee compounded of equal layers of noodles and saltpeter, I was enabled to stay abed mornings where, by covering my head with a pillow, I was no longer inflamed by the sight of the Malaysian beauties.

Since Cameron Highlands was the scene of one of Asia's great unsolved enigmas, the disappearance of James Thompson in 1967 that created international speculation, I was naturally eager to ascertain local opinion of the affair. Thompson, a onetime member of the OSS, famed for his development of Thailand's silk-weaving industry, was visiting friends here one weekend when he suddenly vanished off the face of the earth. Despite continuing search, no clue to his fate has ever turned up, though rumors still circulate of his presence in Peking, India, and elsewhere. As an added grisly complication, his sister, resident on the Main Line outside Philadelphia, was slain soon afterward together with one of her guard dogs—a case that has also defied solution. The manager of my hotel—whose name, predictably, was Mr. Wiseacre—was full of conjectures, none of which struck me as valid. He did, however, provide one interesting crumb of information.

"You know the last thing Thompson did before he disappeared?" he said. "He took along his passport, documents, and all his money. People just don't do that when they go for a walk in the Malaysian jungle. That man *planned* to drop out—don't tell me."

I didn't, but I mentioned it subsequently to a journalist friend in Singapore, who scoffed and countered with a rationale of the mystery worth consideration. Thompson, not too familiar with the terrain, was probably unaware that the forest around Cameron Highlands concealed illegal tiger and bear traps, pits full of sharpened bamboo stakes set by the aborigines. Any natives finding his body clearly would be terrified of being implicated in the death of a white *tuan*, and would have taken jolly good care no trace of him would ever be found. Having seen some of these fierce little folk and their blowguns around Brinchang and Tanah Rata in the Highlands, I was inclined to agree with the theory. They reminded me of nothing so much as that fearsome creation of Conan Doyle's, the Andaman Islander with the poisoned darts in *The Sign of the Four*.

Just as the average girl in my youth dreamt of one day owning a Baker electric and a kolinsky cape, I had a vision of myself in my twilight years clad in a canary-colored box coat and twirling a malacca cane, entering Reisenweber's with Rosemary Theby on my arm. Gone now, alas, were the bounteous Rosemary and Reisenweber's, but my twilight years were incontestably here, and Malacca, said my guidebook, was only an hour away by air, so it was incumbent on me— nay, imperative—to acquire that cane. Well, you know how those sentimental journeys always pan out. Either the guidebook was outmoded or Malacca had moved; anyway, after three days of arduous travel and verminous beds, I got there and I can speak with authority. There are no malacca canes in Malacca. There is, though, a plenitude of old tombstones and open drains, and for any sociology major seeking underfed Portuguese children, lassitude, and hundred-degree humidity, it is a veritable cornucopia. Perhaps its outstanding feature was a Chinese department store retailing nine kinds of peanut butter, more varieties of English cookies than exist at Fortnum's, licorice from every country in Europe, and a huge stock of aphrodisiacs, love philters, and girlie magazines. This seemed bizarre merchandise for a poverty-stricken Malaysian community at the back of beyond until I learned that an RAF base had once existed close by. The panoply of porn, or pornoply so to speak, also accounted for a lovely genetic mutation—a rash of fair-haired Chinese babies—that would have perplexed the father of the Mendelian theory, to say nothing of their own fathers.

Hong Kong, the world's mightiest bazaar—Hong Kong, whose dissonant theme song blends the ring of the cash register with the metronome click of the abacus—once more I was under the Union Jack, crossing the bay on the Star Ferry to hoist a jar with my beloved friend and dean of the press corps, Richard Hughes, Australia's gift to the gaiety of nations. Steaming through the busy harbor traffic of sampans, junks, and water taxis, the billion candlepower of Victoria's skyscrapers, Wanchai, and the Peak aglow in the dusk, I beheld the parade of countless freighters lying in the roads and felt that sense of homecoming the great port always evokes. Hughes, dear man, was unchanged, as ever; his cheeks flamed like pippins and his monocle glittered with the same ferocity as he touched on the decrease of cats in Peking under the People's Republic, the spread of neuroparalysis among television viewers, and kindred ravages of the age.

"But enough in this somber strain, your grace," he broke off. "You too have endured much since we broke bread last—the hurly-burly of life in New York, the intrigues and jealousies of the theater, the silken caresses of designing women. Naught appears to have left a mark on you or silvered your raven locks."

"With one dire exception, Dick. Right after we parted in 1972, the plane carrying me to the outback in your native land was hijacked at Alice Springs."

"I read of that mishap in the blats. Instinct told me you behaved with your usual sangfroid."

"No," I confessed. "There was one moment, when that psychopathic swine leveled his Armalite at my gederma, that I became so choked with fury I was tempted to wrest the weapon from his grasp."

"What prevented you?"

"The club sandwich I was eating. I was afraid I might swallow the toothpick."

"Bravo," he commended me. "You're the stuff bookkeepers are made of—and me too. Well, serves you right for being in Australia—the savages have taken over." He clapped his hands and an obsequious Celestial bore in a wine cooler. "*Permesso*, monsignor. Let us fill our cups with the sparkling Falernian and pledge confusion to the enemies of the Crown—in particular, all the mushmouthed diplos, half-baked gurus, female chauvinists, and Communist running dogs tirelessly bent on castrating us."

It was an Arcadian idyll, those eight days in Hong Kong, the more so since I resolutely forbore doing everything that custom regards as obligatory there. I ate no lobster fresh-plucked from the briny deep in its floating restaurants, bought not a pearl or bead of mutton-fat jade at warehouse prices. I spurned all entreaties to garb me in cashmere, hooted at bargains in embroidered linens, camphor chests, and ingenious ivory balls-within-balls, and ruthlessly averted my gaze from those sloe-eyed Chinese lovelies fragile as porcelain. For let's face it, gang, I was beat. Six months on the road and too many airline meals had taken their toll; I needed a sanctuary where I could knit up the ravell'd sleave of care, and I unearthed one. The virtues of the Peninsula in Kowloon have been extolled far and wide, but I can add one more. Unlike too many posh hotels nowadays, it contains no deluxe suites named after celebrities, literary or otherwise. Which, if nothing else, makes it a haven that deserves to be spelled with an extra "e."

"What'll it be this evening, sir—the usual grenadine and water?" the barman asked as I entered his domain for a farewell draught.

"No, make it a brandy smash, George," I told him with an important cough. "Fact is, I'm off to Borneo in the morning—Kota Kinabalu, Brunei, Kuching, the lot. Yes, sir, this time tomorrow I'll be in The Land Below the Wind."

"Where the head-hunters roam, eh?" He chuckled. "Rum place that, Borneo. Full of Dyak pirates, blackwater fever, people without heads . . . "

"That's all changed today," I assured him loftily. "Bo Goldwasser, who runs the travel agency I deal with on Madison Avenue, explained that the people used to be primitive—"

"Well, he'd know, of course," the barman conceded. "I only spent eleven years there. But if I were you, friend, I'd have my head exam—I mean, insured—before I leave here. Just a precaution. That drink taste all right?"

I licked my lips. "I—I don't know. It's kind of salty."

"That's because you're crying into it," he said kindly. "Must be some sort of allergy, like the one I have toward Borneo. Why don't you lie down for a while and see what happens?"

I did. I went upstairs, fell into the kip, and next morning flew to Java instead. It just goes to show how a chance encounter can sometimes save a person's neck. If I've learned one thing, it's that you've got to be flexible when you travel.

8

To One Cup of Java, Add One Snootful of Tahiti

"Excuse me, sir, excuse me, please!" the frantic young Indonesian in the Pierre Cardin suit besought me. "Are you the Cindy Pemmican from Hong Kong I'm supposed to meet here? Or is your name Sandy Perkomalt, by any chance?"

"Sorry—it's not." The heat in the Jakarta airport lounge was devastating and his feverishness if anything intensified it. "What does the passenger you want look like?"

"Search me," he replied distractedly. "It's an author of some kind—the teletype didn't say. An American scribbler, I believe."

I winced at the appellation but let it pass. "Well, Cindy and Sandy are girls' names—like Cindy Adams and Sandy Dennis. Still, it *could* be a transsexual." I scanned the arrival area. "I can't spot any here, but why not page them and see what turns up?"

His voice rose, reedy with desperation. "How can I when I'm not sure of the name? All I know is there's a suite waiting for someone at the Jakarta Stilton with complimentary fruit!"

"Wait a minute," I said, struck by a sudden thought. I drew out my passport and examined it. "It says here my name's Sidney Perelman and that I'm a writer. Now you mention it, some press agent in Hong Kong did offer me a free pad at the Stilton complete with fruit. Could I be the party you're looking for?"

"Well, you're close enough," he said reluctantly. "Of course, if the real person shows up, you'll have to vacate and return the fruit. You understand that?"

"Oh, sure, sure, I won't make any trouble," I said and followed him to a limousine drawn up outside. "So the hotel is very crowded, is it?"

The question obviously startled him. "Well—er—just between us, it isn't even built yet."

"I don't read you," I said. "Where am I supposed to sleep, then—in the blueprints?"

"No, no, you're in the bomb-proof executive lanais—those are ready for occupancy. So is the Tycoonery, the dining room reserved for VIPs, as well as the archery range and a special sauna for dogs and cats. However, the twelve hundred rooms for the general public won't be finished until 1985—in fact, we may never build them at all. We want this to be the most exclusive hotel in Asia."

I promised that, come 1985, I would fly in my wheelchair to attend the premiere and write a cover story for *Time*. Exultant at the prospect of publicity, he began extolling the wealth of poppy seeds in the Tycoonery's breakfast rolls, the detergents used to launder its towels, and other features of consuming interest to newsmen. Midway through his litany, we reached the thirty-five-acre tract where the skeleton of the future hostel reared up like an unfinished Tinker Toy. I was conducted through a maze of subterranean passages to my executive burrow, in which the decorator, by a skillful use of heavy parchment lampshades and fifteen-watt bulbs, had achieved almost Stygian darkness. The furniture, designed in purportedly Batak style from Sumatra, was so incrusted with warts, knobs, and gingerbread that I bled like a stuck pig while unpacking. This was trifling, however, compared to my search for the highly acclaimed fruit, a cluster of overripe mangoes and bananas. After ransacking the closets and stripping the beds, I finally unearthed it in the chandelier, shrouded in cellophane, but fury and fatigue had eroded my appetite and I flung the blasted thing into the loo.

I number among my friends several ladies who, as a result of seeing Janet Leigh liquidated in Alfred Hitchcock's *Psycho,* have never since been able to enter a shower. My overnight stay at the Jakarta Stilton, oddly, produced the same neurosis, though without mayhem. Hardly was I out of the shower and lathered up to shave when the wall above the bathtub sagged forward and dozens of tiles rained down with a roar like the Victoria Nyanza Falls (The Smoke That Thunders). As I leaped sideways into the bedroom, it came to me with horrid clarity that had I lingered under the spray, I would have suffered the fate the Chinese call the Death of a Thousand Cuts. When my knees ceased trembling sufficiently to pick up the phone—an action I normally perform with my hands, but fright had immobilized them—I aroused the manager, a Javanese aptly named Mr. Nauseatrauma. Following a prolonged study of the debris, he rendered his opinion. Either the tiles had been dislodged by an earthquake, a cataclysm the hotel was not legally responsible for, or else my excessive use of hot water had dissolved the gutta-percha bonding them to the wall—in which case I could expect to pay through the nose, as sure as God made little green express checks. His bland countenance betrayed no hint of coercion, but in my mind's eye there arose a vision of myself, skinnier than a potato chip, stitching mailbags in an Indonesian hoosegow. Yielding to *force majeure*, I reached for my fountain pen.

At three pip emma that afternoon, I sat rigidly in the tonneau of an asthmatic 1956 Chevrolet crawling up-country toward Bandung in the central highlands. The trip, which I had been dreading for weeks, was the outcome of a promise rashly given an acquaintance in London the year before. Eric Fassnidge owned a small art gallery off Bond Street specializing in the work of naïve and primitive painters. An intense, darkly handsome fellow with Byronic features, he was a man of many talents, not the least of which was inveigling naïve and primitive females into the Fruit-of-the-Loom. Along with this, unhappily, went an inability to extricate himself; three of his bedfellows, having lost their naïveté, dragged him to the altar, and finally, plagued by alimony, Fassnidge sold his shop and fled to Java. In a euphoric moment I had consented to visit him there, and now my chickens were coming home to roost. What folly had possessed me to sojourn with a man I hardly knew? Anyone fatuous enough to marry three women was unstable to begin with; by now he might well be a raving lunatic. I lashed myself mercilessly for my soft-heartedness.

As I anticipated, it was a grueling journey, punctuated by endless detours, a broken fan belt, and a minor collision with a gravel truck. To further twist the knife, my driver, a borderline cretin with a head carved out of a Hubbard squash, strayed off the route, and I was denied the one solace I hoped for—a glimpse of the world-famed Buitenzorg botanical gardens at Bogor. By the time we found our way to the quarter of Bandung Fassnidge resided in, night had fallen, frogs were croaking, and the household showed not a glimmer of light. In response to continued knocking, a bearded figure wearing a turban and smoked glasses peered out. He was holding a parang, the type of machete Indonesians employ for gardening and disemboweling.

"Fassnidge? Fassnidge?" he quavered in a falsetto. "Nobody here by that name, tuan. We are poor humble folk, tillers of the soil—"

"Damn it all, Fassnidge, what is this charade?" *107*

I demanded. "I'm your American friend from London—don't you remember your invitation? Open up!"

"Oh, it's Pelican," he said with a sigh of relief. "I didn't recognize you, Sinbad. Come in, come in." He fumbled the chain off the door. "One can't be too careful with all the leeches around."

Crowding past him into the foyer, I watched mystified as he removed the paraphernalia disguising his face. My instinct was right; the chap was crazy as a potato bug and would have to be handled with kid gloves. "What leeches do you mean, old man?" I inquired gently.

"Process servers—bill collectors—the devil knows what they are!" he rasped. "Everything was fine till those hags I married in England hired a solicitor to trace me—and now I sit here like a frozen robin while they bleed me white." He uttered a savage laugh. "Ha ha! Well, they're mistaken, the vampires—I've got a trick or two up my sleeve!"

"Of course you have," I soothed him, and pushed away the parang he was waving. "Look, I really must turn in—five hours on the road—"

"Don't you want something to eat first? I've got a pork dish in the fridge that's a bit moldy, but you can cut away the green parts."

"I like the green parts."

"So did I," he said eagerly. "That was the trouble with my third wife, she never let me eat them. Boy, the stories I'm going to tell you . . . "

Providentially, I remembered in time the old
Malay maxim "He who sups with a paranoiac

conjugates a breakdown," and cut him short. Assigning me the chamber next to his own with an injunction not to fret if he paced the floor all night, Fassnidge withdrew. I sat down on the bed to consider my options. If I tried to escape via the front door, the rattle of the bolts and chain would creat a ruckus. To set fire to the bedclothes and stamp it out, generating enough smoke to cover my flight, was equally impractical. That left but one alternative—the windows—and here luck was with me; though two had been nailed shut, I succeeded in prying open the third with my pocketknife, at the cost of a few dismal squeaks. Kissing my Saint Christopher medal, I thrust my weekend bag over the sill and squirmed after it. A heavy dew sprinkled the turf outside and fireflies blinked in the starlight, but not a sound issued from the house. A wave of exultation swept over me. Now all I had to do was negotiate the 173 kilometers back to Jakarta.

Once to every mortal, when the skein of his destiny seems hopelessly entangled, the knots unravel and he discerns the answer to all his problems. Such a moment of revelation came to me the next morning an hour before dawn. "How comes it that a shell of a man like yourself, a tissue of infirmities, sits huddled in a cold rain on a truckful of cabbages plodding to market in northwestern Java?" I catechized myself. "Will this exercise in masochism, worthy of inclusion in Foxe's Book of Martyrs, conceivably benefit mankind or add by one scintilla to its store of knowledge?" "No, and I'll tell you why not," I replied. "Because you are a slippered pantaloon and a romantic dunce. Except for some shattered tiles in a bathtub and a smudge in your passport, you've come through the Indonesian archipelago with a whole skin—so quit complaining and use your open ticket to Tahiti. Have your forgotten your daydreams of Tahiti—its glorious beaches, its blue lagoons edged by feathery palms, its languorous dusky maidens, its simple and unspoiled populace?" "All right already, I *heard* you," I snapped. "I'll go see the airline as soon as we're back in Jakarta. Meanwhile, let's see if I can't get some sleep on top of these cabbages."

I got precious little, but I managed to redress the balance on a Qantas jet southbound to Sydney, where yet another lofted me onward to Nandi in Fiji and thence to Papeete. Aboard the latter, thanks to a gossipy little news sheet called *Coconut Radio* published in California, I was given a preview of goings-on in Tahiti. At the Hotel Bora Bora, it recounted, "The girls of the dinning room (where the din, presumably, was unparalleled) are so Tahitian and some of the original employees are still here—including Leah, who is awaiting her seventh baby—Evelyne and Cecile, to name a few." In the 1975 annual fete, I learned, "the exhausting Fruit Carrying Race was won by Tiny Tinamano, a beautifully conditioned athlete." That cheered me up immensely; so it was not spleen, but lack of coordination, that had impelled me to cast that fruit into the loo at the Stilton. "A tragic fire has destroyed Papeete's only pool hall," the paper went on. "It is rumored they will not rebuild but create a parking lot instead." Disturbing news this, for left without a pool hall to loaf around, Papeete's loafers might well turn ugly and foment a revolution. Still, there were plenty of cool heads to forestall such a contingency, as a final item demonstrated: "A team of Tahitian store owners have visited the New Hebrides Islands to investigate the possibility of importing their corned beef product. After much can-opening and tasting, they returned to Papeete to discuss." Yes, I concluded, all in all, the mixture of din, fruitful waitresses, revolution, and corned beef promised an eventful holiday.

The promise was fulfilled, and amply. The Royal Polynesian Arms, the rookery I was lodged in fronting the harbor, abutted on a dry-cleaning plant, so that I awoke mornings not to the heady scent of bougainvillea and frangipani, but bathed in steam, inhaling the smell of frying cloth. The tourist diversions offered me, however, were manifold and cheap. I could dally with a Pepsi in numerous quaint bars whose management graciously supplied me a ten-foot pole with which not to touch the fat Tahitian hookers ogling me. I could make daily tours on foot, with a fair chance of sunstroke, to four banks where, amid guffaws at my French accent, I was apprised that the exchange rate on the dollar had fallen. Cruising the myriad stalls along the waterfront, I could also ascertain what needed no verification, that thousands of shell necklaces were manufactured in

Pawtucket, Rhode Island, for export. Failing all these, I could take a bus to Maeva Beach, tie two lumps of coral to my feet, and wade out till my nose submerged. I was debating just this form of felo-de-se one noon when fate, in the person of a distinguished old Frenchman, intervened.

"*Bonjour, monsieur.*" The white goatee and Windsor tie at the café table adjoining mine, the rumpled velvet jacket and the brushes protruding from his beret, bespoke an artist. "You are an American, *peut-être?* Permit me to introduce myself—Paul Gauguin, a painter by profession."

I took his proffered hand. "The name has a familiar ring."

"Yes, my daubs enjoy a small local celebrity, possibly because I have lived here so long. Since 1889, in fact, when, tired of life in France as a stockbroker, I deserted my wife and children and came here to limn the natives."

"How are you prospering?"

"Oh, passably, save for a touch of elephantiasis now and then. Anyhow, now that we are old friends, I can speak without reserve. I require a small loan of eleven thousand francs—about $2750 in your money."

"Not in my money, lover," I said. "You're singing down an empty rain barrel. What do you need it for—canvases and paint?"

"No, a down payment on a Toyota and a new set of threads," he said. "I'm trying to make out with a wahine I met, a chick with a dynamite figure, but I can't get to first base with my present image. O.K., then—can we talk a deal?"

My eyes narrowed. "Nobody ever got burned by listening."

"Right." He looked around stealthily. "That dame near the coffee machine with the blue rinse and breloque-style diamond earrings—she's loaded. Can we play her for the gypsy switch?"

"You mean, mingle our dough with hers to make it grow and she winds up with some shredded newspaper? Brother," I said scornfully. "Even Richard Nixon would be ashamed to pull that one."

"Hell, I'm just spitballing a few ideas," he placated me. "How about this? You take her out bathing while I glom the jewelry in her room. Then I'll fence it in Guam or Samoa and send your cut to L.A."

"I like it, Paul, I *like* it," I said, chewing it over, "but now I'm going to put wings on it, so listen closely. You dress up like a priest, see, and you marry us."

"You mean, you and me?" he said startled.

"No stupid, me and the dame," I said impatiently. "Step number two—I've insured her for two hundred grand and we sail for Hawaii on our honeymoon. Unbeknownst to her, you're on the ship dressed as a sailor and you push her overboard. I collect the insurance in Honolulu and send your cut to Tokyo."

"But how do I get to Tokyo?" he protested fretfully. "I can't even pay for this vermouth I just had. If you could lend me twelve francs—I'll bring it around to your hotel tomorrow—"

I dusted off my trousers and arose. "Please, 113

monsieur," I said icily, "desist, I beg of you. Whereas I visualized a golden dream of two devil-may-care scamps like Robert Redford and Paul Newman in *The Sting*, you saw nothing but a sordid touch for coffee money. If that is what civilization has done to Tahiti, I want none of it. Farewell."

And that is how I left Papeete, heavy in heart, light in purse, and sick with disillusion. Behind me lay a whited sepulcher entombing the fantasies Pierre Loti, Herman Melville, and Nordhoff and Hall had kindled in my breast. But ahead, just over the horizon, loomed the spires of the Great Pueblo, the City of Our Lady the Queen of the Angels, daring me to scale them. Did I have the pluck, the grit it entailed? Flexing my sinews, I deadened nerves and stomach with a gill of Stolichnaya and prepared to meet the challenge.

9

Back Home in Tinseltown

Under a blond pompadour whose wavelets lapped a forehead narrower than Ronald Reagan's, the cabdriver's smile was pure maple sugar and the schmaltz in his voice unrivaled in Southern California. "That'll be nine dollars and a half, buddy. Have a good day."

I recoiled as though hit in the posterior with a baked apple. "Nine bucks from the Beverly Wilshire to Hollywood and Vine? I could have got here for a quarter on the bus!"

"Sure, if you like riding with wetbacks and sheenies," he agreed. "Speaking as a member of the John Birch Society—"

"No need to identify yourself," I cut him short. I know a *Judenfresser* when I see one. "This is an outrage—a rip-off!"

"Look, Grandpa, don't blow your pacemaker," he said. "You asked the doorman for a radio cab—right? I picked up the call in Sherman Oaks,

so you bleed for my trip back. Hand it over—
we're holding up traffic."

I thrust two singles through the hatch. "There's
your gelt, you chiseler," I said, "and I'm reporting
you to the next cop I see." As he bent down to
reach for a tire-iron, I noticed with a start that the
chap had no neck whatever, merely a knot of
muscle like an orangutan's. My wrath turned to
shame. I had mocked a cripple. "Gee, I'm sorry,
friend. Can you break a twenty?"

"Gladly, sir," he replied, all aggression flown. I
naturally rewarded him with a generous tip and
disembarked glowing with self-approbation.
Prior to this eight-month journey around the
world, I would have lost my temper and blacked
the man's eye. Today, ripened and matured by
travel, I had become more saintly and compassionate than Velvet Joe, as mellow as an old
winesap. How fitting, therefore, that the trip
should conclude with a sentimental revisit to the
birthplace, forty-five years before, of my career as
a screenwriter. Yes—it was on this very spot, at
the conflux of Hollywood Boulevard and Vine
Street, that I had taken my first enchanted foot-
steps into the temple of the silver screen.

Time, I shortly discovered, had wrought
changes in the renowned thoroughfare. Its side-
walks now gleamed with stars embodying the
names of various players through whose artistry
millions of cinemagoers had achieved catharsis,
each name a certified cathartic—Greer Garson,
Kenny Baker, Vera Hruba Ralston, Paul Henreid,
Dyan Cannon, Elliott Gould. There was, however,

no decline of witlessness in the flicks at the local picture houses; still available to kiddies from six to sixty was a nosegay that included *Texas Chain Saw Massacre*, *Sizzling Topless Widows*, and *Boys in Their Nest Agree*. A porno shop with a dazzling inventory of sexual cacti bloomed between Vine and Ivar, outside it a band of young *exaltés* chanting appeals to passersby to spurn its wares. Of the high-class ladies' specialty stores I recalled, some had become outlets for see-through bikinis, others haberdasheries for transvestites, and the remainder peepshows for erotomaniacs, interspersed with fast-food restaurants guaranteeing instant botulism. Yet, curiously enough, the human tide flowing sluggishly by me was unchanged. If many were Hare Krishnas, a sect of loafers undreamt of in the thirties, most of the pedestrians were the same old screwballs and screwboxes—losers of beauty contests, Texas gigolos, nature fakers, shoe salesmen and similar voyeurs, absconding bank cashiers, unemployed flagellants, religious messiahs, and jail bait. Did there exist anywhere, I wondered, a Hogarth or a Hieronymus Bosch who could do justice to these satanic troglodyte faces preoccupied with unimaginable larcenies and *Schweinerei?* As if in answer to my thoughts, the incredible happened. Voices called to me from a sleek Cadillac at the curb and I descried the countenances of Marty Hogarth and Anonymous Bosch, a pair of television writers out of my past.

"Hell's bells, man, this is kid stuff," they scoffed on learning of my research. "Hop in and we'll show you the real Camembert." A quick transit southward brought us to the County Strip, an enclave on Santa Monica Boulevard between Hollywood and Los Angeles. It was fringed by half a dozen educational foundations bearing such names as the Institute of Oral Love, Climax Prep, Dr. Unameit's School of Ecstasy, and Bondage Unlimited. Their pedagogues, a group of lovelies whose necklines revealed them to be stacked like buckwheat cakes, were evidently on sabbatical, since they were crouched in doorways grooming each other's hides for fleas and puffing on reefers. Eager to impart their knowledge, however, they swarmed about us offering special private tutelage and free Wassermanns. I was particularly charmed by one establishment whose sign read, "Wrestle a Naked Lady—Ten Dollars Back If You Win." Had my companions ever accepted the challenge, I inquired?

"Yeah, twice," Hogarth confessed sheepishly. "I lost both times."

Our appetites longing for more and madder wine, the three of us adjourned to a booth at Le Gangster, Beverly Hills' ranking French restaurant, where we dallied exchanging gossip and sipped egg creams laced with Mouton Rothschild. The handful of my Hollywood contemporaries still alive, Bosch divulged, were enjoying a pleasurable second childhood. They busied themselves coloring comic books, played with stage money doled out by their business managers, and occasionally, as an extra treat, were permitted to drool on television.

"And their spouses?" I inquired. "What has become of those stunning, long-legged showgirls, goddesses ransomed from Ziegfeld and Earl Carroll, with whom one used to play footsie under the dinner tables?"

"They too have undergone a magic rebirth, thanks to Dr. Ana Aslan and procaine," he said. "Many of them, sporting second and third faces, are here this moment, escorted by Filipino cicisbeos whose consciousness and other adjuncts the ladies help to raise periodically at Esalen."

"That is heartening news," I said. "Judging from this new awareness, would you say that Hollywood is moving into another Golden Age resembling the thirties?"

"Incontestably," Hogarth responded, quenching his cigar in the butter. "The old rough-and-tumble era when junkmen and furriers like Louis B. Mayer and Adolph Zukor dominated the industry is no more. Nowadays your average producer is a bookworm, a brainy, highly sensitive collegian holding degrees from Paine Whitney, Riggs, and other cultural centers. Contemptuous of hacks like Harold Robbins and Irving Wallace, he keeps his finger on the public throat, seeking themes that will elevate as well as entertain. Did you know, for instance, that M-G-M's entire product next season is based on a forthcoming series of books by Sheilah Graham?"

"About what?"

"Well, it seems that while cleaning out a thimble she discovered still more revelations anent that tortured spirit Scott Fitzgerald. Paramount,   119 not to be outdone, has bought A. E. Hotchner a Ouija board to assist him in exhuming further idiosyncrasies of Hemingway's."

"Graham and Hotchner better lay low when Truman Capote hears of this," commented Bosch. "Left without any more jet-set peccadillos to disclose, he may sue them for restraint of trade or even scratch their eyes out."

"Nonsense," I rejoined. "Shucks, there's a wealth of juicy screen material in the past, real gamy stuff, that Hollywood's ignored. Why doesn't some producer latch on to Aubrey's *Brief Lives* or the diary of Samuel Pepys? Think of the adulteries in those chronicles, the wenching, the steamy indiscretions—"

"Hold on there, you," a voice broke in. The speaker, a bronzed and bearded diner in a persimmon-colored bush jacket whose cleavage exposed a chestful of Tibetan amulets, was bending over me threateningly. "I'm Monroe Sweetmeat of Subcutaneous Pictures. I overheard that crack you made about my friend."

"What friend?"

"Aubrey—the former production chief at CBS and Metro. You said he wrote a book filled with steamy indiscretions."

"No, no, *he* didn't write it. Someone else did."

"You mean this someone else ghosted it and Aubrey took the credit?"

I threw up my hands. "How could he, for Pete's sake? The real Aubrey, the one I'm talking about, died three hundred years ago."

120   "Oh, then you're calling my friend a fake Au-

brey, are you?" he rasped. "Take that back or I'll
knock your block off!"

"You will, will you?" I sprang up, doubling
my tiny fists. "Maybe my two colleagues'll have
something to say about that." Receiving no assur-
ance from the twain, I peered around mystified;
they had apparently slipped out during our con-
frontation. Just as I was preparing to faint, Sweetmeat's ire subsided as quickly as it had arisen.

"Wait a second," he enjoined, retrieving Hogarth's cigar from the butter. "If what you say is
so, then the rights to that book are in the public
domain. Nobody could prevent me from making
a picture out of it."

"There might be an estate, though," I pointed
out. "Maybe you ought to take it up with their
lawyer."

"No, I prefer to steal the property direct," he
said, and scratched his amulets thoughtfully.
"Still and all, the Samuel Pepys diary sounds like
it might have more pizazz. Get a copy over to my
office this afternoon so I can read it." I assured
him that all eight volumes, complete with foot-
notes, would be there without fail. "Are there any
hard words in it?"

"I don't think so. Just a few scatological ex-
pressions."

"No problem. My secretary, which she graduated from a college down on Santa Monica Boulevard, knows more about scat than Ella Fitzgerald."
As we issued from the restaurant, he draped an
arm familiarly over my shoulder. "What did you
say your name was?"

"Seymour J. Weasel, of Hornblower and Weasel. Our agency is new in these parts, Mr. Sweetmeat, but whatever your needs in literary chicanery, I'm confident we can supply them."

"Sy, it's a pleasure to do business with you," he said, settling into his Bentley Sedanca de Ville with body work by Mulliner. I was exultant, and small wonder. Within the space of minutes, such is the loose and easy camaraderie of show business that I had come to know a powerful, influential figure I would never have to see again as long as I lived, God willing.

Given the leisure, I would have liked to dawdle in the movie colony; Indian summer was nigh, with the promise of flaming color from the fires and mud slides in its canyons that annually draw thousands of tourists to Vermont. The truth was, though, that I had an obligation that outweighed all else—an obligation which, were I to avoid it, would have broken faith with someone who meant the world to me. The perceptive reader will already have guessed that I had been shafted by Dan Cupid, the blind bowboy, and such was the case, but can he visualize my angel, Gabrielle de Casabas, as I first caught sight of her thirty-six hours before aboard the aircraft winging home from Tahiti? Can he credit that her low-cut black jersey dress concealed a figure as sumptuous as Sophia Loren's, that her hair was spun gold, her mouth a scarlet wound and her scent more delicious than asphodel, that she embodied all I had ever longed for in woman? Irony of ironies, even

I was unaware of it, for I was too deeply engrossed in a talk on poultry diseases in my earphones to notice the vision of loveliness seated beside me. Once I noticed it, off came the earphones.

"Mademoiselle," I said without preamble, "you see before you one who has girdled the globe six times in vain looking for perfection. Despite all the pundits, it is not at Angkor Wat or the Taj Mahal. Nor is it in the Louvre, the Metropolitan, or the Hermitage."

"Indeed." I read no more than a flicker of interest in her great violet eyes. "Then I should give up if I were you."

"I have," I said, taking her hand. "I found it here, in my own back yard. I must have you."

"You must have me?" Her gaze became troubled. "But you cannot, monsieur. I belong to another."

"Who is it?" I demanded fiercely. "Tell me his name and I'll kill him. You think I'm joking? I was never so serious in my life."

"*Tiens*," she said. "Aren't you being rather impetuous?"

I uttered a savage laugh. You think *that's* impetuous? Then watch this," I said, and set my lips in a grim line. "Have you ever seen such a stubborn little mouth?"

Well, as it turned out she never had, so, accepting defeat gracefully, she consented to pour out her story. The only child of a bankrupt diamond dealer in Antwerp, she had nevertheless won a scholarship at the Lycée Condorcet, received her baccalaureate in philosophy at the Sorbonne, and come to Altoona, Pennsylvania, to learn English, having been advised that the brand spoken there was the purest to be found in the States. While vacationing at South Fallsburg in the Catskills, she made the acquaintance of a young man employed, so he said, as a floorwalker at Neiman-Marcus in Dallas.

"What did I know of the world?" she said bitterly. "I was naïve, gullible, a romantic. All too soon his true identity emerged. The scion of a prominent Santa Barbara family, he boasted a string of polo ponies, drank to excess, and beat me unmercifully. I have an aversion to wealth, a phobia I must have inherited from my father—"

"I also," I put in, squeezing her hand. More and more, as her tale unfolded, it became clear what a community of interests we shared.

"*Enfin*, things grew so intolerable between us that at Jackson Hole, Wyoming, where we had gone to water his ponies, I made the decision to flee to the South Seas and cleanse myself of him. There, lying on the talcum-white sands of Maeva Beach in Papeete, I realized how I had been taken advantage of."

"I also," I said. "Do you know what those French bastards charged me?"

"Hush," she said, laying a finger on my lips. "Soon, restored by the healing sun and surf, it dawned on me that I had been questing after false gods. Possibly he whom I sought to insure my happiness did not exist, yet already I could discern his outlines. Far from a great hulking brute like Nick, he must be a shrimp, an introvert, a sport in the strict biological sense. Fuzzy in garb as well as mentality, restless, waspish, opinionated, I saw a rover who loathed nothing more than puttering around his home workshop, a man who knew how to treat a whore like a lady and vice versa. In short, a free-lance writer with bushy eyebrows and dim prospects peering through little oval glasses."

I arose jubilantly, dusted my trousers, and sank down on one knee—no mean achievement in economy class. "My treasure, I speak without consulting the Guinness Book of Records. Nevertheless, I believed this to be the only clean proposal ever made at thirty-seven thousand feet. Will it be accepted?"

"Rise, impetuous boy," she breathed, blushing like a peony. "Don't you know that from the moment I secured my seat belt, the outcome was never in doubt?"

And so it came to pass that one week later, in the patio of Marty Hogarth's home in Coldwater Canyon, Gabrielle and I exchanged vows mingling our community property. Amid the babble of the guests and the explosion of champagne corks, I confessed to myself that my feelings were mingled as well. Triumph, to be sure, that out of this nettle, Hollywood, I had plucked this flower, but mixed with it, a tinge of apprehension. Tomorrow, my peregrination of the planet complete, the flower and I would be back in Fun City,

where every prospect freezes the blood and only
man is vile. Oh, well, kid, I decided, drink up—
you win a little, you lose a little. Isn't that what
it's all about?